POWER
for you

POWER
for you

CHARLES SPURGEON

Whitaker House

All Scripture quotations are from the *King James Version* (KJV) of the Bible.

POWER FOR YOU

ISBN: 0-88368-379-2
Printed in the United States of America
Copyright © 1996 by Whitaker House

Whitaker House
580 Pittsburgh Street
Springdale, PA 15144

1 2 3 4 5 6 7 8 9 10 11 / 06 05 04 03 02 01 00 99 98 97 96

Contents

Chapter 1

The Outpouring of the Holy Spirit

While Peter yet spake these words, the Holy Ghost fell on all them which heard the word.
—Acts 10:44

The Bible is a book of the revelation of God. The God after whom the heathen blindly searched and for whom reason gropes in darkness is here plainly revealed to us in the pages of divine authorship. He who is willing to understand as much of the Godhead as man can know may here learn it if he is not willingly ignorant and willfully obstinate.

The doctrine of the Trinity is specially taught in Holy Scripture. The word "trinity" certainly does not occur, but the three divine persons of the one God are frequently and constantly mentioned. Holy Scripture is exceedingly careful that we should all receive and believe that great truth of the Christian religion: the Father is God, the Son is God, and the Spirit is God. Yet, there are not three gods but one God. Though they each are very God of very God, three in one and one in three is the Jehovah whom we worship.

You will notice in the works of Creation how carefully the Scriptures assure us that all three divine persons took their share. "In the beginning God created the heaven and the earth" (Gen. 1:1). In another place, we are told that God said, "Let *us* make man in *our* image" (Gen. 1:26). It was not one person but all three taking counsel with each other with regard to the making of mankind. We know that the Father has laid the foundations and fixed those solid beams of light on which the blue arches of the sky are sustained. But, we know with equal certainty that Jesus Christ, the eternal Logos, was with the Father in the beginning, and "without him was not any thing made that was made" (John 1:3). Moreover, we have equal certainty that the Holy Spirit had a hand in Creation, for we are told that "the earth was without form, and void; and darkness was upon the face of the deep. And the Spirit of God moved upon the face of the waters" (Gen. 1:2). Brooding with His dove-like wing, He brought out of the egg of chaos this mighty thing—the fair, round world.

We have like proof of the three persons in the Godhead in the matter of salvation. We know that God the Father gave His Son. We have abundant proof that God the Father chose His people from before the foundation of the world, and He invented the plan of salvation. He has always given His free, willing, and joyous consent to the salvation of His people.

With regard to the share that the Son had in salvation, that is apparent enough to all. For us men and for our salvation, He came down from heaven. He was incarnate in a mortal body. He was crucified, died, and was buried. He descended into hell, and on the third day He rose again from the dead. He ascended into heaven, and He sits at the right hand of God where He also makes intercession for us.

As to the Holy Spirit, we have equally sure proof that the Spirit of God works in conversion, for everywhere we are said to be created by the Holy Spirit. It is continually declared that unless "a man be born again [from above], he cannot see the kingdom of God" (John 3:3). All the virtues and the graces of Christianity are described as being the fruits of the Spirit because the Holy Spirit works from first to last in us and carries out that which Jesus Christ has beforehand worked for us in His great redemption. God the Father has also designed this for us in His great predestining scheme of salvation.

Now, it is the work of the Holy Spirit that I wish to especially direct to your attention, and I may as well mention the reason why I do. It is this: in the United States of America, there has been a great awakening.[1] Two hundred and fifty thousand people profess to have been regenerated. They have united themselves with different sections of God's church. What makes me believe that the work is genuine is this: the enemies of Christ's holy Gospel are exceedingly angry at it. When the devil roars at anything, you may rest assured that there is some good in it. The devil is not like some dogs we know of; he never barks unless there is something to bark at. When Satan howls, we may rest assured that he is afraid his kingdom is in danger.

Now, this great work in America has been manifestly caused by the outpouring of the Spirit, for no one minister has been a leader in it. All the ministers of the Gospel have cooperated in it, but none of them have stood at the forefront. God Himself has been the leader of His own hosts. It began with a desire for prayer. God's people began to pray, and the prayer meetings were better attended than

---

[1] The great revival of 1858, afterwards experienced in Britain.

before. It was then proposed to hold meetings at times that had never been set apart for prayer; these also were well attended. Plus, there has been real prayer. Sinners, beyond all count, have risen up in the prayer meetings and have requested the people of God to pray for them. They thus made public to the world that they had a desire for Christ. They have been prayed for, and the church has seen that God truly does hear and answer prayer.

Now, to have a similar effect produced in this land, the one thing we must seek is the outpouring of the Holy Spirit. I thought that perhaps my writing about the work of the Holy Spirit might fulfill the text, "Them that honour me I will honour"(1 Sam. 2:30). My sincere desire is to honor the Holy Spirit, and if He will be pleased to honor His church in return, unto Him will be the glory forever.

While Peter yet spake these words, the Holy Ghost fell on all them which heard the word.   (Acts 10:44)

In the first place, I will endeavor to describe the method of the Spirit's operation. Secondly, I will demonstrate the absolute necessity of the Holy Spirit's influence if we would see men converted. Thirdly, I will suggest the ways and means by which, under divine grace, we may obtain a like outpouring of the Spirit upon our churches.

The Method of the Holy Spirit's Operations

As I discuss the method of the Holy Spirit's operations, let me guard myself against being misunderstood. We can explain what the Spirit does, but how He does it no man must pretend to know. The work of the Holy Spirit is the peculiar mystery of the Christian religion. Almost any other thing is plain, but this must remain an inscrutable secret into which it is wrong for us to attempt to pry. Who knows where the winds come from? Who knows, therefore, how the Spirit works, for He is like the wind? "The wind bloweth where it listeth, and thou hearest the sound thereof, but canst not tell whence it cometh, and whither it goeth: so is every one that is born of the Spirit" (John 3:8). I take it that the Holy Spirit's work in conversion is twofold. First, it is an awakening of the powers that man already has, and secondly, it is an implantation of powers which he never had at all.

In the great work of the new birth, the Holy Spirit first of all awakens the mental powers—remember that the Holy Spirit never gives any man new mental powers. Take, for instance, reason; the Holy Spirit does not give men reason for they have reason prior to their conversion. What the Holy Spirit does is to teach our reason, to set our reason on the right track, so that we can use it for the high purpose of discerning between good and evil, between the precious and vile. The Holy Spirit does not give man a will because man has a will before, but He makes the will that was in bondage to Satan free to the service of God. The Holy Spirit gives no man the power to think or the organ of belief, for man already has power to believe or think as far as the mental act is concerned; however, He gives that belief which is already there a tendency to believe the right thing, and He gives to the power of thought the propensity to think in the right way. Then, instead of thinking irregularly, we begin to think as God would have us think, and our minds desire to walk in the steps of God's revealed truth.

There may be reading this a man of enlarged understanding in things political, but his understanding is darkened with regard to spiritual things. He sees no beauty in the person of Christ. He sees nothing desirable in the way of holiness. He chooses the evil and forsakes the

13

good. Now, the Holy Spirit will not give him a new understanding, but He will cleanse his old understanding so that he will discern between things that differ. He will then discover that it is but a poor thing "to enjoy the pleasures of sin for a season" (Heb. 11:25) and forgo an "eternal weight of glory" (2 Cor. 4:17). There may also be a man reading this who is desperately set against religion and will not come to God. Do what we will, we are not able to persuade him to change his mind and turn to God. The Holy Spirit will not make a new will in that man, but He will turn his old will. He will make him willing to do right instead of willing to do evil. He will make him willing to be saved by Christ; He will make him "willing in the day of thy power" (Ps. 110:3).

Remember, there is no power in man so fallen that the Holy Spirit cannot raise it up. However debased a man may be, in one instant by the miraculous power of the Spirit, all his faculties may be cleansed and purged. Ill-judging reason may be made to judge rightly. Stout, obstinate will may be made to run willingly in the ways of God's commandments. Evil and depraved affections may in an instant be turned to Christ, and old desires that are tainted with vice may be replaced by heavenly aspirations. The work of the Spirit on the mind

14

is the remodeling of it, the new forming of it. He does not bring new materials to the mind—it is in another part of the man that He puts up a new structure—but He puts the mind that had fallen out of order into its proper shape. He builds up pillars that had fallen down and erects the palaces that had crumbled to the earth. This is the first work of the Holy Spirit upon the mind of man.

Besides this, the Holy Spirit gives to men powers which they never had before. According to Scripture, I believe man is constituted in a three-fold manner. He has a body; by the Holy Spirit that body is made the temple of the Lord. He has a mind; by the Holy Spirit that mind is made like an altar in the temple. But man by nature is nothing higher than that; he is mere body and soul. When the Spirit comes, He breathes into him a third, higher principle which we call the spirit. The apostle describes man as, "spirit and soul and body" (1 Thess. 5:23).

Now, if you search all the mental writers through, you will find they all declare there are only two parts, body and mind. They are quite right, for they deal with unregenerate man, but in regenerate man there is a third principle as much superior to mere mind as mind is superior to dead animal matter. That third principle is that with which a man prays; it is that with which he savingly believes. It is that which compels the mind to perform its acts. It is that which, operating upon the mind, makes the same use of the mind as the mind does of the body. When, after desiring to walk, I make my legs move, it is my mind that compels them. So my spirit, when I desire to pray, compels my mind to think the thought of prayer; it compels my soul also, if I desire to praise, to think the thought of praise and lift itself upward towards God. As the body without the soul is dead, so the soul without the spirit is dead, and one work of the Spirit is to quicken the dead soul by breathing into it the living spirit. As it is written, "The first man Adam was made a living soul; the last Adam was made a quickening spirit" (1 Cor. 15:45) and, "as we have borne the image of the earthy, we shall also bear the image of the heavenly" (1 Cor. 15:49). That is, we must have in us, if we would be converted, the quickening spirit which is put into us by God the Holy Spirit.

I say again, the spirit in us has powers which the mind never has. It has the power of communion with Christ which to a degree is a mental act, but it can no more be performed by man without the spirit than the act of walking could be performed by man if he were destitute of a soul to suggest the idea of walking. The spirit suggests the thoughts of communion which the mind obeys and carries out. There are times, I think, when the spirit leaves the mind altogether, times when we forget everything of earth, and one almost ceases to think, to reason, to judge, to weigh, or to will. Our souls are like the chariots of Amminadib (see Song of Solomon 6:12), drawn swiftly onwards without any powers of volition. We lean upon the breast of Jesus, and in rhapsody divine and in ecstasy celestial, we enjoy the fruits of the land of the blessed and pluck the clusters of Eshcol before entering into the land of promise. (See Numbers 13:23–24; Deuteronomy 1:24–25.)

I think I have clearly put these two points before you. The work of the Holy Spirit consists, first, in awakening powers already possessed by man but which were asleep and out of order, and in the next place it consists in putting into man powers which he did not have before. To make this simple to the humblest mind, let me suppose man to be something like a machine; the wheels are out of order, the cogs do not strike upon each other, the wheels do not turn regularly, the rods will not act, and the order is gone. Now, the first work of the

Spirit is to put these wheels in the right place, to fit the wheels upon the axles, to put the right axle to the right wheel, and then to put wheel to wheel so that they may act upon each other. But that is not all of His work. The next thing is to put fire and steam so that these things will go to work. He does not put on fresh wheels; He puts old wheels into order, and then He puts the motive power which is to move the whole. First, He puts our mental powers into their proper order and condition, and then He puts in a living, quickening spirit so that all these will move according to the holy will and law of God.

And I must say, before I leave this point, that all the former part of what I have mentioned is done instantaneously. When a man is converted to God, it is done in a moment. Regeneration is an instantaneous work. Conversion to God, the fruit of regeneration, occupies all our lives, but regeneration itself is effected in an instant. A man hates God; the Holy Spirit makes him love God. A man is opposed to Christ; he hates His Gospel, does not understand it, and will not receive it. The Holy Spirit comes, puts light into his darkened understanding, takes the chain from his bondaged will, gives liberty to his conscience, and gives life to his dead soul so that the voice of conscience is heard. Then the man becomes a new creature in Christ Jesus. And all this is done, mark you, by the instantaneous, supernatural influence of God the Holy Spirit working as He will among the sons of men.

The Absolute Necessity of the Spirit's Work in Order to Convert

In our text we are told that "while Peter yet spake these words, the Holy Ghost fell on all them which heard the word" (Acts 10:44). Beloved, the Holy Spirit fell on Peter first or else it would not have fallen on his hearers. There is a necessity that the preacher himself, if we are to have souls saved, should be under the influence of the Spirit. I have constantly made it my prayer that I might be guided by the Spirit even in the smallest and least important parts of the service, for you cannot tell if the salvation of a soul may depend upon the reading of a hymn or upon the selection of a portion of Scripture. Two people have joined our church and made a profession of being converted simply through my reading the hymn: "Jesus, Lover of My Soul."

They did not remember anything else in the hymn, but those words made such a deep impression upon their minds that they could not help repeating them for days afterwards, and then the thought arose, "Do I love Jesus?" And then they considered what strange ingratitude it was that He should be the lover of their souls and yet they should not love Him. Now, I believe the Holy Spirit led me to read that hymn. Many people have been converted by some striking saying of the preacher, but why was it the preacher uttered that saying? Simply because he was led thereunto by the Holy Spirit.

Rest assured, beloved, that when any part of the sermon is blessed to your heart, the minister said it because he was ordered to say it by his Master. I might preach a sermon today that I preached on Friday which was useful then, but no good whatever will come from it now because it might not be the sermon that the Holy Spirit would have delivered today. But, if with sincerity of heart I have sought God's guidance in selecting the topic and if He rests upon me in the preaching of the Word, there is no fear that it will not be found adapted to the hearers' immediate wants.

The Holy Spirit must rest upon your preachers. Even if he has all the learning of the wisest men and all the eloquence of such men as Demosthenes and Cicero, still the Word cannot be blessed to you unless first of all the

Spirit of God has guided the minister's mind in the selection of his subject and in the discussion of it. However, if Peter himself were under the hand of the Spirit, that would fail unless the Spirit of God then did fall upon his hearers, and I will endeavor now to show the absolute necessity of the Spirit's work in the conversion of men.

Let us remember what kind of thing the work is, and we will see that other means are altogether out of the question. It is quite certain that men cannot be converted by physical means. The Church of Rome thought that it could convert men by means of armies, so it invaded countries and threatened them with war and bloodshed unless they would repent and embrace its religion. However, it availed but little, and men were prepared to die rather than leave their faith. It therefore tried such beautiful things—stakes, racks, dungeons, axes, swords, fire—and by these things it hoped to convert men.

You have heard of the man who tried to wind up his watch with a pick ax. That man was extremely wise compared with the man who thought to touch mind through matter. All the machines you like to invent cannot touch mind. Talk about tying angels' wings with green twigs or manacling the cherubim

with iron chains, and then talk about meddling
with the minds of men through physical
means. Why, the things don't act; they cannot
act. All the king's armies that ever were and
all the warriors clothed with mail with all their
ammunition could never touch the mind of
man. That is an impregnable castle which is
not to be reached by physical agency.

Nor, again, can man be converted by moral
argument. "Well," says one, "I think he may.
Let a minister preach earnestly, and he may
persuade men to be converted." Ah, beloved, it
is for want of knowing better that you say so.
Melanchthon thought so, but you know what
he said after he tried it: "Old Adam is too
strong for young Melanchthon." So will every
preacher find it, if he thinks his arguments can
ever convert man.

Let me give you a parallel case which is
drawn from Jeremiah 13:23. Where is the logic
that can persuade an Ethiopian to change his
skin color? By what argument can you induce a
leopard to renounce his spots? Even so may he
that is accustomed to do evil learn to do well.
But if the Ethiopian's skin is to be changed, it
must be by supernatural process, and if the
leopard's spots are to be removed, He that
made the leopard must do it. Even so is it with
the heart of man. If sin were a thing *ab extra*

(literally, from the outside) and external, we could induce man to change it. For instance, you may induce a man to leave off drunkenness or swearing because those things are not a part of his nature; he has added that vice to his original depravity. But the hidden evil of the heart is beyond all moral persuasion. I dare say a man might have enough argument to induce him to hang himself, but I am certain no argument will ever induce him to hang his sins, to hang his self-righteousness, and to come and humble himself at the foot of the cross. The religion of Christ is so contrary to all the propensities of man that it is like swimming against the stream to approach it, for the stream of man's carnal will and man's desire is exactly the opposite of the religion of Jesus Christ.

I have seen the tears run down a man's cheeks when he has come to me in order to be united to the church of Christ, and he has said, "Sir, I wonder how it is I am here today; if anyone had told me a year ago that I should think as I now think and feel as I now feel, I should have called him a born fool for his pains. I liked to spend my Sunday in pleasure, and I did not see why I was to be cooping myself up in the house of God listening to a man talk. *I* pray, sir? No, not I. I said the best providence in all the world was a good strong pair of hands and to take care of what you got. If any man talked to me about religion, why, I would slam the door in his face and pretty soon put him out. But the things that I loved then, I now hate, and the things that then I hated, now I love. I cannot do or say enough to show how total is the change that has been wrought in me. It must have been the work of God; it could not have been wrought by me, I feel assured. It must be someone greater than myself who could thus turn my heart."

I think these things are proofs that we want something more than nature. Since physical agency will not do and mere moral persuasion will never accomplish it, there must be an absolute necessity for the Holy Spirit.

But again, if you will just think a minute what the work is, you will soon see that none but God can accomplish it. In the Holy Scripture, conversion is often spoken of as becoming a new creation. (See 2 Corinthians 5:17; Galatians 6:15.) If you talk about creating yourselves, I should feel obliged if you would create a fly first. Create a gnat, create a grain of sand, and when you have created that, you may talk about creating a new heart. Both are alike impossible, for creation is the work of God. But still, if you could create a grain of dust or create even a world, it would not be half the miracle, for you must first find a thing which has created itself. Could that be? Suppose you had no existence—how could you create yourself? Nothing cannot produce anything. Now, how can man recreate himself? A man cannot create himself into a new condition when he has no being in that condition but is, as yet, a thing that is not.

Then, again, the work of creation is said to be like the resurrection. We "are alive from the dead" (Rom. 6:13). Now, can the dead in the grave raise themselves? Let any minister who thinks he can convert souls go and raise a corpse. Let him go and stand in one of the cemeteries and bid the tombs open wide their mouths and make room for those once buried there to awaken, and he will have to preach in vain. Even if he could do it, that is not the miracle we are addressing; rather, it is for the dead to raise themselves, for an inanimate corpse to kindle in its own breast the spark of life anew. If the work is a resurrection, a creation, does it not strike you that it must be beyond the power of man? It must be wrought in him by no one less than God Himself.

And there is yet one more consideration, and I will have concluded this point. Beloved, even if man could save himself, I would have you recollect how averse he is to it. If we could make our hearers all willing, the battle would be accomplished. "Well," says one, "if I am willing to be saved, can I not be saved?" Assuredly you can, but the difficulty is, we cannot make men to be willing. That shows, therefore, that there must be a constraint put upon their wills. There must be an influence exerted upon them, which they have not in themselves, in order to make them willing in the day of God's power.

This is the glory of the Christian religion which has within its own bowels power to spread itself. We do not ask you to be willing first. We come and tell you the news, and we believe that the Spirit of God working with us will make you willing. If the progress of the Christian religion depended upon the voluntary assent of mankind, it would never go an inch further; however, because the Christian religion has with it an omnipotent influence, constraining men to believe it, it is therefore what it is and must be triumphant until like a sea of glory it spreads from shore to shore.

What Must be Done at This Time in Order to Bring Down the Holy Spirit

It is quite certain, beloved, if the Holy Spirit willed to do it, that every man, woman, and child reading this might be converted now. If God, the Sovereign Judge of all, would be pleased now to send out His Spirit, every inhabitant of this million-peopled city might be brought at once to turn unto the living God. Without instrumentality, without preachers, without books, without anything, God has it in His power to convert men. We have known people about their business, not thinking about religion at all, who have had a thought injected into their hearts, and that thought has been the prolific mother of a thousand meditations through which they have been brought to Christ. Without the aid of a minister, the Holy Spirit has thus worked, and today He is not restrained. There may be some men, great in infidelity, staunch in opposition to the Cross of Christ; without asking their consent, the Holy Spirit can pull down the strong man and make the mighty man bow himself. For when we talk of the omnipotent God, there is nothing too great for Him to do.

But, beloved, God has been pleased to put great honor upon instrumentality. He could work without it if He pleased, but He does not do so. However, this is the first thought I want to give you; if you would have the Holy Spirit exert Himself in your midst, you must first of all look to Him and not to instrumentality.

When Jesus Christ preached, there were very few converted under Him, and the reason was that the Holy Spirit was not abundantly poured forth. He had the Holy Spirit without measure Himself, but on others the Holy Spirit was not as yet poured out. Jesus Christ said, "Greater works than these shall he do; because I go unto my Father" (John 14:12), in order to send the Holy Spirit. Recollect that those few who were converted under Christ's ministry were not converted by Him but by the Holy Spirit that rested upon Him at that time. Jesus of Nazareth was anointed by the Holy Spirit. Now then, if Jesus Christ, the great founder of our religion, needed to be anointed by the Holy Spirit, how much more do our ministers need this anointing?

And now, another thought. If we would have the Spirit, beloved, we must each of us try to honor Him. There are some chapels into which, if you were to enter, you would never know there was a Holy Spirit. Mary Magdalene said of old, "They have taken away my Lord, and I know not where they have laid him" (John 20:13). The Christian also might often say so, for there is nothing said about the Lord until they come to the end of the service, and then there is just the benediction. Without this benediction, you would not know that there were three persons in one God at all. Until our churches honor the Holy Spirit, we will never see it abundantly manifested in our midst. Let the preacher always confess before he preaches that he relies upon the Holy Spirit. Let him burn his manuscript and depend upon the Holy Spirit. If the Spirit does not come to help him, let him be still, and let the people go home and pray that the Spirit will help him next Sunday.

And do you also, in all of your work, always honor the Spirit? We often begin our religious meetings without prayer; it is all wrong. We must honor the Spirit. Unless we put Him first, He will never make crowns for us to wear. He will get victories, but He will have the honor of them. If we do not give to Him the honor, He will never give to us the privilege and success. And best of all, if you would have the Holy Spirit, let us meet together earnestly to pray for Him. Remember, the Holy Spirit will not come to us as a church unless we seek Him. "I will yet for this be inquired of by the house of Israel, to do it for them" (Ezek. 36:37). "Prove me now herewith, saith the LORD of hosts, if I will not...pour you out a blessing, that there shall not be room enough to receive it" (Mal. 3:10).

Let us meet and pray, and if God does not hear us, it will be the first time He has broken

His promise. Come, let us go up to the sanctuary; let us meet together in the house of the Lord and offer solemn supplication. I say again, if the Lord does not make bare "his holy arm in the eyes of all the nations" (Isa. 52:10), it will be the reverse of all His previous actions; it will be contrary to all His promises and contradictory to Himself. We have only to try Him, and the result is certain. In dependence on His Spirit, if we only meet for prayer, the Lord will bless us, and all the ends of the earth will fear Him.

Oh, Lord, lift up Yourself because of Your enemies; pluck Your right hand out of Your bosom, oh, Lord our God, for Christ's sake, Amen.

Chapter 2

The Holy Spirit Compared to the Wind

*"The wind bloweth where it listeth, and thou
hearest the sound thereof, but canst not tell
whence it cometh, and whither it goeth: so is
every one that is born of the Spirit."*
—John 3:8

I am not proposing to enter fully into the subject of the new birth but to bring before you the parallel which our Savior here draws between the wind and the Holy Spirit. It is a remarkable fact, known I dare say to most of you, that both in the Hebrew and Greek languages the same word is used for spirit and for wind so that our Savior, as it were, rode upon the wings of the wind while he was instructing the seeking Rabbi in the deep things of God. He caught at the very name of the wind as a means of fastening a spiritual truth upon the memory of the inquirer, hinting to us that language should be watched by the teacher that he may find out suitable words and employ those which will best assist the disciple to comprehend and to retain his teaching.

"The wind," said He, "bloweth," and the very same word would have been employed if He had meant to say, "The Spirit bloweth where He listeth." There was doubtlessly intended to be a very close and intimate parallel between the Spirit of God and the wind, or otherwise the great Ruler of providence, who invisibly controlled the confusion of Babel, would not have fashioned human language so that the same word would stand for both. Language, as well as nature, illustrates the wisdom of God.

It is only in His light that we see light. May the Holy Spirit be graciously pleased to reveal Himself in His divine operations to all our waiting minds. We are taught in God's Word that the Holy Spirit comes upon the sons of men and makes them new creatures. Until He enters them, they are "dead in trespasses and sins" (Eph. 2:1). They cannot discern the things of God because divine truths are spiritual and spiritually discerned, and unrenewed men are carnal and possess not the power to search out the deep things of God. The Spirit of God creates anew the children of God. Then, in their newborn spirituality, they discover and come to understand spiritual things, but not before. Therefore, my beloved hearers, unless you possess the Spirit, no metaphors, however simple, can reveal Him to you. Let us not mention the name of the Holy Spirit without due honor. Forever blessed be You, most glorious Spirit, coequal and coeternal with the Father and with the Son; let all the angels of God worship You! Be had in honor, world without end!

In What Sense May the Holy Spirit Be Compared to the Wind

The Spirit of God, to help the spiritually minded in their study of His character and nature, condescends to compare Himself to dew, fire, oil, water, and other suggestive types. Among the rest, our Savior uses the metaphor of wind. What was the first thought here but that of mystery? It was the objection to the point of mystery which our Lord was trying to remove from the mind of Nicodemus. Nicodemus in effect said, "I cannot understand it; how can it be? A man born again when he is old, created over again, and that from an invisible agency from above? How can these things be?" (See John 3:4, 9.) Jesus at once directed his attention to the wind, which is nonetheless real and operative, because of its mysterious origin and operation.

You cannot tell where the wind comes from. You know it blows from the north or from the west, but at what particular place does that wind start on its career? Where will it pause in its onward flight? You see that it is blowing to the east or to the west, but where is its halting-place? Where did these particles of air that rush so rapidly past come from? Where are they going? By what law are they guided in their course, and where will their journey end? The gale may be blowing due east here, but it may be driving west a hundred miles away. In one district the wind may be rushing from the north, and yet not far from it there may be a strong current from the south. If you have watched the skies, you must occasionally have noticed a stream of clouds hurrying to the right, while higher up another company is sailing to the left.

The philosopher may scheme some conjecture to prove that the trade winds blow at certain intervals because of the sun crossing the equator at those periods and that there must necessarily be a current of air going towards the equator because of the rarefaction, but he cannot tell you why the weathercock on yonder church steeple turned this morning from southwest to due east. He cannot tell me why it is that the sailor finds that his sails are at one time filled with wind, and in a few minutes they fall loosely about so that he must steer upon another tack if he would make headway. The various motions of the air remain a mystery to all but the infinite Jehovah.

My fellow Christians, the like mystery is observed in the work of the Spirit of God. His person and work are not to be comprehended by the mind of man. He may be present now, but you cannot see Him. He speaks to one heart, but others cannot hear His voice. He is not recognizable by the unrefined senses of the unregenerate. The spiritual man discerns Him, feels Him, hears Him, and delights in Him, but neither wit nor learning can lead a man into the secret. The believer is often bowed down with the weight of the Spirit's glory or lifted up upon the wings of His majesty, but even he knows not how these feelings are wrought in him.

The fire of holy life is at seasons gently fanned with the soft breath of divine comfort, or the deep sea of spiritual existence stirred with the mighty blast of the Spirit's rebuke. But still, it is evermore a mystery how the eternal God comes into contact with the finite mind of His creature man, filling all heaven meanwhile and yet dwelling in a human body as in a temple—occupying all space and yet operating upon the will, the judgment, and the mind of the poor, insignificant creature called man.

We may inquire, but who can answer us? We may search, but who will lead us into the hidden things of the Most High? He brooded over chaos and produced order, but who will tell us after what fashion He wrought the pattern? He overshadowed the Virgin and prepared a body for the Son of God, but into this secret who will dare to pry? His is the anointing, sealing, comforting, and sanctifying of the saints, but how does He work all these things? "He maketh intercession for the saints according to the will of God" (Rom. 8:27). He dwells in us and leads us into all truth, but who among us can explain to his fellows the order of the divine working? Though veiled from human eye like the glory which shone between the cherubim, we believe in the Holy Spirit and therefore see Him, but if our faith needed sight to sustain it, we should never believe at all.

Mystery is far from being all which the Savior would teach by this simile. Surely He meant to show us that the operations of the Spirit are like the wind for divinity. Who can create a wind? The most ambitious of human princes would scarcely attempt to turn, much less to send forth the wind. These steeds of the storm know no bit or bridle, neither will they come at any man's bidding. Let our senators do what they will, they will scarcely have the madness to legislate for winds. Old Boreas, as the heathens called him, is not to be bound with chains and welded on earthly anvil or in vulcanian forge. "The wind bloweth where it listeth" (John 3:8), and it does so because God directs it and suffers it not to halt for man or to tarry for the sons of men. So it is with the Spirit of God. All the true operations of the Spirit are due in no sense whatever to man but always to God and to His sovereign will.

Revivalists may get up excitement with the best intentions and may warm people's hearts until they begin to cry out, but all this ends in nothing unless it is divine work. Have I not said scores of times in the pulpit, "All that is of nature's spinning must be unraveled?" Every particle which nature puts upon the foundation will turn out to be but "wood, hay, stubble" (1 Cor. 3:12) and will be consumed. It is only "gold, silver, precious stones" (1 Cor. 3:12) of God's building that will stand the fiery test. "Ye must be born again" (John 3:7) from above, for human regenerations are a lie. Yo may blow with your mouth and produce some trifling effects upon trifles as light as air. Man in his zeal may set the windmills of silly minds in motion, but, truly, to stir men's hearts with substantial and eternal verities, a celestial breeze such as the Lord alone can send is needed.

Did not our Lord also intend to hint at the sovereignty of the Spirit's work? For what other reason did He say, "The wind bloweth where it listeth" (John 3:8)? There is an arbitrariness about the wind; it does just as it pleases, and the laws which regulate its changes are unknown to man. "Free as the wind," we say, "the wild winds." So is the mighty working of God. It is a very solemn thought, and one which should tend to make us humble before the Lord, that we are, as to the matter of salvation, entirely in His hand! If I have a moth in my hand right now, I can bruise its wings or crush it at my will, and by no attempts of its own can it escape from me. And every sinner is absolutely in the hand of God, and, let him recollect, he is in the hand of an angry God, too. The only comfort is that he is in the hand of a God who, for Jesus' sake, delights to have mercy upon even the vilest of the vile.

Sinner, God can give you the Holy Spirit if He wills. But if He should say, "Let him alone," your fate is sealed; your damnation is sure. Do you tremble at this? Do you cry, "Oh, God, have pity upon me"? He will hear your cry, sinner, for there never yet was a sincere cry that went up to heaven, though it were ever so feeble, that did not have an answer of peace. When one of the old saints lay dying, he could only say, "Oh, Lord, I trust you *languida fide,*" with a languid faith. That is poor work, but, oh, it is safe work. You can only trust Christ with a feeble faith. If it is such a poor, trembling faith that it does not grip Him but only touches the hem of His garment, it nevertheless saves you. If you can look at Him, though it be only a great way off, it saves you anyway. And, oh, what a comfort this is, that you are still on pleading terms with Him and in a place of hope. "He that believeth on him is not condemned" (John 3:18).

But, oh, do not trifle with the day of grace, unless having frequently heard the warning and hardened your neck just as often, you should "suddenly be destroyed, and that without remedy" (Prov. 29:1), for if He shuts out, none can bid you to come in. If He slides the iron bar closed, you are shut out in the darkness of obstinacy, obduracy, and despair forever, the victim of your own delusions. Sinner, if God saves you, He will have all the glory, for

He has a right to do as He will because He says, "I will have mercy on whom I will have mercy, and I will have compassion on whom I will have compassion" (Rom. 9:15).

Still I think I have not yet brought out what is in the text. Do you not think that the text was intended to show the varied methods in which the Spirit of God works in the conversion and regeneration of men? "The wind bloweth where it listeth" (John 3:8). Now, observe the different force of the wind. This afternoon the wind seemed as if it would tear up every tree; doubtless, had they been in leaf, many of those noble princes of the forest would have stretched themselves prone upon the earth. But, God takes care that in these times of boisterous gales there should be no leaf. Therefore, the wind gets but little purchase with which to uproot a tree.

However, the wind does not always blow as it did this wintry afternoon. On a summer's evening there is such a gentle zephyr that even the gnats who have been arranging a dance among themselves are not disturbed but keep to their proper places. Yes, the aspen seems as if it could be quiet, though you know it keeps forever quivering, according to the old legend that it was the tree on which the Savior hung and, therefore, trembles still as though through

40

fear of the sin which came upon it. This is but a legend. There are times when all is still and calm, when everything is quiet, and you can scarcely detect the wind at all.

Now, just so it is with the Spirit of God. To some of us, He came like "a rushing mighty wind" (Acts 2:2). Oh, what tearings of soul there were then! My spirit was like a sea tossed up into tremendous waves, made, as Job says, "to boil like a pot" (Job 41:31) until one would think the deep were ancient. Oh, how that wind came crashing through my soul, and every hope I had was bowed as the trees of the wood in the tempest. Read the story of John Bunyan's conversion; it was just the same. Turn to Martin Luther; you find his conversion of the same sort. So might I mention hundreds of biographies in which the Spirit of God came like a tornado sweeping everything before it, and the men could but feel that God was in the whirlwind.

To others He comes so gently that they cannot tell when first the Spirit of God came. They recollect that night when mothers prayed so with brothers and sisters and when they could not sleep for hours because the big tears stood in their eyes on account of sin. They recollect the Sunday schools and the teachers there. They remember that earnest minister.

They cannot say exactly when they gave their hearts to God, and they cannot tell about any violent convictions. They are often comforted by that text, "One thing I know, that, whereas I was blind, now I see" (John 9:25), but they cannot get any farther. They sometimes wish they could. Well, they need not wish it, for the Spirit of God, as a sovereign, will always choose His own way of operation. If it is the wind of the Holy Spirit, recollect it is as saving in its gentleness as in its terror, and it is as efficient to make us new creatures when it comes with the zephyr's breath as when it comes with the hurricane's force. Do not quarrel with God's way of saving you. If you are brought to the cross, be thankful for it; Christ will not mind how you got there. If you can say, "He is 'all my salvation, and all my desire' (2 Sam. 23:5)," you never came to that without the Spirit of God bringing you to it. Do not therefore think you came the wrong way, for that is impossible.

Again, the wind not only differs in force, but it differs in direction. We have been saying several times the wind is always shifting. Perhaps there never were two winds that did blow exactly in the same direction. I mean that if we had power to detect the minute points of the compass, there would be found some deviation in every current; although, of course, for all practical purposes, it blows from certain distinct points which the mariner marks out. Now, the Spirit of God comes from different directions. You know very well, dear friends, that sometimes the Spirit of God will blow with mighty force from one denomination of Christians; then all of a sudden they seem to be left, and another body of Christians God will raise up, fill with Himself, and qualify for usefulness. In the days of Wesley and Whitefield, there was very little of the divine Spirit anywhere except among the Methodists. I am sure they do not have a monopoly of Him now.

The divine Spirit blows also from other quarters. Sometimes He uses one man, sometimes another. We hear of a revival in the North of Ireland; by and by it is in the South of Scotland. It comes just as God wills for direction, and you know, too, dear friends, it comes through different instrumentalities in the same church. Sometimes the wind blows from the pulpit; God blesses a preacher to your conversion. Another time it is from a good sister's prayer group; on a third occasion it is the Sunday school. Again, it may be another class or the preaching of the young men or from the individual exertion of private believers. God causes that wind to blow just which way He wills.

He works also through different texts of Scripture. You were converted and blessed under one text; it was quite another that was made useful to me. Some of you were brought to Christ by terrors, others of you by love, by sweet wooing words. The wind blows as God directs. Now, dear friends, whenever you take up a religious biography, do not sit down and say, "Now I will see whether I am just like this person." Nonsense! God never repeats Himself. Men make steel pens—thousands of grosses of them—all alike, but I will be bound to say that in quills from common feathers, there are no two of them precisely the same. If you look, you will soon discover that they differ in a variety of ways.

Certain gardeners cut their trees into the shapes of animals and a number of other unnatural forms, but God's trees do not grow that way. They grow just anyway; they gnarl their roots and twist their branches. Great painters do not continually paint the same picture again and again and again, and my Divine Master never puts His brush on the canvas to produce the same picture twice.

Every Christian is a distinct work of grace on God's part, which has in it some originality, some portion distinct from all others. I do not believe in trying to make all history uniform. It is said that Richard III had a humpback. Whether he really was deformed or whether history gave him the humpback I cannot tell, but it is said that all his courtiers thought it the most beautiful humpback that ever was seen. And they all began to grow humpbacks, too. I have known ministers who had some peculiar idiosyncrasy of experience which was nothing better than a spiritual humpback, but their people all began to have humpbacks, too—to think and talk all in the same way and to have the same doubts and fears. Now, that will not do. It is not the way in which the Most High acts with regard to the wind, and if He chooses to take all the points of the compass and make use of them all, let us bless and glorify His Name.

Are not the different winds various in their qualities? Few of us like an east wind. Most of us are very glad when the wind blows from the south. Vegetation seems to love the southwest much. A stiff northeaster is enough to make us perish, and long continuance of the north wind may well freeze the whole earth. While from the west, the wind seems to come laden with health from the deep blue sea, and though sometimes too strong for the sick, it is never a bad time when the west wind blows.

The ancients all had their different opinions about wind: some were dry; some were rainy; some affected this disease; some touched this part of men; some the other. It is certain that God's Holy Spirit has different qualities. In the Song of Solomon, He blows softly with the sweet breath of love. Turn on farther, and you get that same Spirit blowing fiercely with threatening and denunciation. Sometimes you find Him convincing the world "of sin, and of righteousness, and of judgment" (John 16:8); that is the north wind. At other times you find Him opening up Christ to the sinner and giving him joy and comfort; that is the south wind that blows softly and gives a balminess in which poor troubled hearts rejoice. Yet "all these worketh that one and the selfsame Spirit" (1 Cor. 12:11).

Indeed, my subject is all but endless, and therefore I must halt my discussion. But even in the matter of duration, you know how the wind will sometimes blow six weeks in this direction and, then, continue in another direction. Likewise, the Spirit of God does not always work with us. He does as He pleases; He comes, and He goes. We may be in a happy hallowed frame at one time, and at another we may have to cry, "Come from the four winds, O breath" (Ezek. 37:9).

The Parallel between the Holy Spirit and the Effects of the Wind

"Thou hearest the sound thereof" (John 3:8). Ah, that we do! The wind sometimes wails as if you could hear the cry of mariners far out at sea or the moanings of the widows that must weep for them. Likewise, the Spirit of God sets men wailing with an exceedingly bitter cry for sin, as one that is in sorrow for his firstborn: "Thou hearest the sound thereof." Oh, it is a blessed sound, that wailing! Angels rejoice over "one sinner that repenteth" (Luke 15:10). Then comes the wind at another time with a triumphant sound, and if there is an Aeolian harp in the window, how it swells, sweeps, descends, then rises again, gives all the tones of music, and makes glad the air with its jubilant notes. So it is with the Holy Spirit; sometimes He gives us faith and makes us bold, full of assurance, confidence, joy, and peace in believing. "Thou hearest the sound" of a full symphony of the Holy Spirit's mighty melody within the soul of man, filling him with peace and joy and rest and love.

Sometimes the wind comes, too, with another sound, as though it were contending. You heard it, perhaps, this afternoon. We who are often in the country hear it more than you do.

It is as though giants were struggling in the sky together. It seems as if two seas of air, both lashed to the point of fury, met and dashed against some unseen cliffs with terrible uproar. The Spirit of God comes into the soul sometimes and makes great contention with the flesh. Oh, what a stern striving there is against unbelief, against lust, against pride, against every evil thing.

"Thou hearest the sound thereof" (John 3:8). You, who know what divine experience means, know when to go forth to fight your sins. When you can hear "the sound of a going in the tops of the mulberry trees" (2 Sam. 5:24) then you stir yourself to smite your sins. Sometimes the wind has come with a sweep as though it were going on forever. It came past and dashed through the trees, sweeping away the rotten branches, then away across the Alps, dashing down an avalanche in its course, still onward. As it flew, it bore away everything that was frail and weak; on, on, on it sped its way to some unknown goal.

Thus it is sometimes that the Spirit of God will come right through us as if He were bearing us away to that spiritual heritage which is our sure future destiny—bearing away coldness, barrenness, everything before it. We do not lament then that we do not pray. We do not believe that we cannot pray, but "I can do all things" (Phil. 4:13) is our joyful shout as we are carried on the wings of the wind. "Thou hearest the sound thereof" (John 3:8). I hope you have heard it sometimes in all its powerful, overwhelming, mighty influence until your soul has been blown away. "Thou hearest the sound thereof."

But then, the wind does something more than make a sound, and so does the Holy Spirit. It works and produces manifest results. Just think what the wind is doing presently. I cannot tell at what pitch it may be. It is just possible that in some part of the ocean a vessel scuds along almost under bare poles; the mariners do their best to reef the sails, but away she goes. Now the mast has gone. They do their best to bear up, but they find that in the teeth of the gale they cannot stand. The ship dashes on the rocks, and she is wrecked.

The Spirit of God is a great wrecker of false hopes and carnal confidences. I have seen the Spirit of God come to a sinner like a storm to a ship at sea. He had to take down the topgallant souls of his pride, and then every thread of carnal confidence had to be reefed. Then his hope itself had to be cut away. And on, on the vessel went, until she struck a rock, and down she went. The man from that time never dared trust in his merits, for he had seen his merits wrecked and broken in pieces by the wind.

The wind, too, recollect, is a great leveler. It always aims at everything that is high. If you are down low in the street, you escape its fury. However, climb to the top of a monument or St. Paul's, and see whether you do not feel it. Get into the valley, and it is all right. The lower branches of the trees are scarcely moved, but the top branches are rocked to and fro by it. It is a great leveler; so is the Holy Spirit. He never sees a man high without bringing him down. He makes every high thought bow before the majesty of His might. If you have any high thought, rest assured that when the Spirit of God comes, He will lay it low even with the ground.

Now, do not let this make you fear the Holy Spirit. It is a blessed thing to be rocked so as to have our hopes tested, and it is a precious thing to have our carnal confidences shaken. How blessedly the wind purifies the atmosphere! In the Swiss valleys there is a heaviness in the air which makes the inhabitants unhealthy. They take quinine, and you see them going about with big swellings in their necks. From Martigny to Bretagne, there is a great valley in which you will see hundreds of people diseased. The reason is that the air does not circulate. They are breathing the same air, or some of it, that their fathers breathed before them. There seems to be no ventilation between the two parts of the giant Alps. The air never circulates, but if they have a great storm which sweeps through the valleys, it is a great blessing to the people. So the Spirit of God comes and cleanses out our evil thoughts and vain imaginations; though we do not like the hurricane, it brings spiritual health to our soul.

Again, the wind is a great trier of the nature of things. Here comes a great rushing up the street. It sweeps over the heaps of rubbish lying in the road; away goes all the light chaff, paper, and other things which have no weight in them. They cannot stand the brunt of its whirling power; but see, the pieces of iron, the stones, and all weighty things are left unmoved. In the country the farmer severed the chaff from the wheat by throwing it up into a current of air; the light husks all blew away while the heavy wheat sank on the heap, cleansed and purified.

So is the Holy Spirit the great testing power, and the result of His operations will be to show men what they are. Here is a hypocrite; he has passed muster hitherto and reckons himself to be a true and genuine man. But here comes a blast from heaven's mighty Spirit, and he finds himself to be lighter than vanity. He has no weight in him; he is driven on and has no rest and can find no peace. He hurries from one refuge of lies to another. "There is no peace, saith my God, to the wicked" (Isa. 57:21).

Thus, also, we try the doctrines of men; we bring the breath of inspiration to bear upon them. Do they abide the test, or are they driven away? Can you hold that truth in the presence of God? Can you cling to it and find it stable in the hour of trial? Is it a nice, pleasant speculation for a sunny day when all is calm and bright, or will it bear the rough, rude blast of adversity when God's Holy Spirit is purifying you with His healthful influence? True Christians and sound doctrines have ballast and weight in them; they are not moved or driven away, but empty professors and hollow dogmas are scattered like chaff before the wind when the Lord will blow upon them with the breath of His Spirit. Examine yourselves, therefore, and try the doctrines to see if they are of God. "What is the chaff to the wheat? saith the LORD" (Jer. 23:28). Have root in yourselves; then you will not wither in the hot blast nor be driven away in the tempestuous day.

The Holy Spirit Compared to the Wind

Is not the Spirit, moreover, like unto the wind in its developing of character? Men get all covered with dust in the hot dusty roadside of life until they are nearly the color of the earth itself, but they come to the hilltop of Calvary and stand here until the wind of heaven has cleansed them from all the dust that has gathered around their garments. Oh, there is nothing like communion with the Spirit of God to counteract the earthly tendencies of a busy life.

There are some men that get covered with a yellow dust until they are almost hidden by it; they can talk of nothing else but money. Gold, gold, gold, occupies nearly every thought. I have no quarrel with money in its right place, but I do not like to see men live for it. I always try to drive away that mean and groveling spirit which lives for nothing else but to accumulate money, but I cannot always succeed. Now, the Spirit of God will make a man see his folly, put his money into its right position, and place the graces of the Christian character where men can see them and glorify God in them. Never let your business character or professional skill dim and hide your Christianity. If you do, God's Spirit will come to brighten you up, and He will have no mercy on these but will, in love for your soul, cleanse and give luster to God's work which is wrought in you.

I see also here a thought as to the cooperation of man and the Spirit in all Christian work. It has pleased God to make us coworkers with Him, fellow laborers, both in the matter of our own salvation and also in the effort to benefit others. Look for a moment at yonder stately sailboat. She moves not because of her sails, but she would not reach the desired haven without them. It is the wind which propels her forward, but the wind would not act upon her as it does unless she had the rigging all fixed, her masts standing, and her sails all bent so as to catch the passing breeze. But, now that human seamanship has done its best, see how she flies! She will soon reach her haven with such a favoring gale as that. You have only to stand still and see how the wind bears her on like a thing of life.

So it is with the human heart. When the Spirit comes to the soul that is ready to receive such influences, He then helps you on to Christian grace and Christian work and makes you bear up through all opposition until you come to the port of peace and can anchor safely there. Without Him we can do nothing; without us He will not work. We are to preach the Gospel to every creature, and while one plants and another waters, God adds the increase (1 Cor. 3:7). We are to work out our own salvation, but He works in us "to will and to do of his good pleasure" (Phil. 2:13).

We must go up to possess the good land with our own spear and sword, but the hornet goes before us to drive out the foe. (See Joshua 24:12.) Jericho will be captured by a divine and miraculous interference, but even there rams' horns will find a work to do and must be employed. The "host of Midian" (Judg. 7:15) will be slain, but our cry is, "The sword of the LORD, and of Gideon" (Judg. 7:18, 20).

We give God all the glory; nevertheless, we use the means. The water of Jordan must be sought out and used by all who desire a cleansing like Naaman the Syrian. (See 2 Kings 5.) A lump of figs must be used if other Hezekiahs are to be healed (see Isaiah 38:21), but the Spirit is, after all, the great Cleanser and Healer of His people Israel. The lesson is clear to all: the wind turns mills that men make and fills sails that human hands have spread, and the Spirit blesses human effort, crowns with success our labors, establishes the work of our hands upon us, and teaches us all through that "the hand of the diligent maketh rich" (Prov. 10:4) but "that if any would not work, neither should he eat" (2 Thess. 3:10).

Another thought suggests itself to my mind in connection with the wind and human effort. It is this: how completely dependent men are upon the wind as to what it will do for them. They are entirely at its mercy as to its time of blowing, its strength, and the direction it will take. I have already dwelled upon this thought of the sovereignty of the wind, but it comes up here in a more practical form. The steamer now can steer almost anywhere it pleases, and at all times it will proceed on its voyage. The sailing ship, however, must tack according to the wind and when becalmed must wait for the breeze to spring up. The sailor who is depending on the wind anxiously looks up to the masthead to see how the breeze is shifting and turning the vane, and he scans the heavens to see what weather he is likely to have. He would not need to care nearly as much as he does when he is absolutely dependent on the wind if he had steam power so as to sail in the very teeth of the storm if he so willed.

God, then, keeps us looking up to heaven by making us to be completely at His mercy as to the times and ways of giving us His helping power. It is a blessed thing to wait on God, watching for His hand and in quiet contentment leaving all to Him. Fellow believers, let us do our part faithfully, spread every sail, make all as perfect as human skill and wisdom can direct, and then in patient continuance in well-doing, wait for the Spirit's propitious gales, neither murmuring because He tarries nor be taken unawares when He comes upon us in His sovereign pleasure to do that which seems good in His sight.

And now, my dear reader, whether you often read my writings or have now stepped in for the first time, I would like to impress this in your heart: Do you know the Spirit of God? If you "have not the Spirit of Christ, [you are] none of his" (Rom. 8:9). "Ye must be born again" (John 3:7).

"What, Lord—'must'? Do You not mean 'may'?" No, you *must*. "Does it not mean, 'You can be'?" No, you *must*.

When a man says, "must," it all depends upon who he is. When God says "must," there it stands, and it cannot be questioned. There are the flames of hell; would you escape from them? You must be born again. There are heaven's glories sparkling in their own light; would you enjoy them? You must be born again. There is the peace and joy of a believer; would you have it? You must be born again. What, not a crumb from off the table without this? No, not one. Not a drop of water to cool your burning tongues unless you are born again. This is the one condition that never moves. God never alters it and never will. You must, *must*, MUST. Which will it be? Shall your will stand or God's will? Oh, let God's "must" ride right over you, and bow yourselves down and say, "Lord, I must, then I will; ah, and it has come to this—I must now. 'Give me Christ, or else I die.'

"I have hold of the knocker of the door of Your mercy, and I *must,* I WILL get that door open. I will never let You go except You bless me. You say *must,* Lord, and I say *must,* too."

You must, "ye must be born again" (John 3:7). May God fulfill the "must" in each of your cases, for Jesus Christ's sake. Amen.

Chapter 3

The Heavenly Wind

The wind bloweth where it listeth, and thou hearest the sound thereof, but canst not tell whence it cometh, and whither it goeth: so is every one that is born of the Spirit.
—John 3:8

The Holy Spirit is to be admired, not only for the great truths which He teaches us in Holy Scripture but also for the wonderful manner in which those truths are balanced. The Word of God never gives us too much of one thing or too little of another. It never carries a doctrine to an extreme but tempers it with its corresponding doctrine. Truth seems to run at least in two parallel lines, if not in three, and when the Holy Spirit sets before us one line, He wisely points out to us the other. The truth of divine sovereignty is qualified by human responsibility, and the teaching of abounding grace is seasoned by a remembrance of unflinching justice. Scripture gives us, as it were, the acid and the alkali, the rock and the oil which flows from it, and the cutting sword and the healing balm. As our Lord sent forth His evangelists two by two, so does He seem to send out His truths two by two, so that each may help the other for the blessing of those who hear them.

Now, in this most notable third chapter of John, you have two truths taught as plainly as if they were written with a sunbeam and taught side by side. The one is the necessity of faith in the Lord Jesus Christ and the fact that "he that believeth on him is not condemned" (John 3:18). This is a vital doctrine, but the Holy Spirit in this chapter lays equal stress upon the necessity of the new birth or the work of the Holy Spirit. He states it quite as plainly as the other grand truth. See how they blend: "Ye must be born again" (John 3:7), but "whosoever believeth in him should not perish, but have everlasting life" (John 3:16). "Except a man be born of water and of the Spirit, he cannot enter into the kingdom of God" (John 3:5), but "he that believeth on him is not condemned" (John 3:18).

Two great truths are written in letters of light over the gate of heaven as the requisites of all who enter there: reconciliation by the blood of Jesus Christ and regeneration by the work of the Holy Spirit. We must not put one of these truths before the other or allow one to obliterate or hide the other. They are of equal importance, for they are revealed by the same divine Spirit and are alike needful to eternal salvation. Faith gives us the rights of the children of God, but the new birth must be experienced so that we may have the nature of children. Of what use would rights be if we did not have the capacity to exercise them?

The Holy Spirit Himself

The figure is the wind, and, as most of you know, the Hebrew word for "wind" and for "spirit" is the same. It is interesting to note that the same is true with the Greek word *pneuma* which signifies both "breath" and "spirit," so that the figure which the Savior used might very naturally grow out of the word which He employed. The wind is air in motion and is, of course, material, but air is apparently more spiritual than any of the other elements except fire since it is not to be grasped by the hand nor seen with the eye. It is certain that wind really exists, for we hear the sound thereof and observe its various effects, but it is not to be touched, handled, or gazed upon. Men cannot traffic in it or measure it in scales or weigh it in balances.

We may watch for hours as we will the clouds as they hasten along like winged fowl, but the wind which drives them is out of our sight. We observe the waves roused to fury in the tempest, but the breath which so excites them we cannot see. Hence, the word "wind" becomes all the more excellent a figure of that mighty power, the Holy Spirit, of whose existence no man who has come under His influence ever doubts. Nevertheless, the Holy Spirit is not to be tracked in His movements or to be seen as to His divine person, for He is mysterious, incomprehensible, and divine.

First, the wind is a figure of the Holy Spirit in its freedom: "The wind bloweth where it listeth" (John 3:8). We speak of the wind as the very image of freedom. We say to those who would enthrall us, "Go bind the winds"; as for ourselves we claim to be "free as the winds which roam at their own will." No one can fetter the wind. Xerxes threw chains into the Hellespont to bind the sea, but even he was not fool enough to talk of forging fetters for the winds. The breezes are not to be dictated to. Caesar may decree what he pleases, but the wind will blow in his face if he looks that way. The Pope may command the gale to change its course, but it will blow around the Vatican neither less nor more for the holy father and the cardinals. A conference of diplomats from all the powers of Europe may sit for a week and resolve unanimously that the east wind will not blow for the next six months, but it will take no heed of the arrangement and will cast dust into the counselors' eyes and whistle at their wisdom. No proclamation or purpose under heaven will be able to affect the wind by so much as half a point of the compass. It will blow according to its own sweet will where it pleases, when it pleases, how it pleases, and as it pleases, for "the wind bloweth where it listeth" (John 3:8).

So it is, only in a far higher and more emphatic sense, with the Holy Spirit, for He is most free and absolute. You know that the wind is in the hand of God and that He ordains every zephyr and each tornado. Winds arise and tempests blow by order from the throne supreme, but as for the Holy Spirit, He is God Himself and absolutely free and works according to His own will and pleasure among the sons of men. One nation has been visited by the Holy Spirit and not another; who will tell me why? Why do yonder heathen lands lie in the dense darkness while in Britain the light is concentrated? Why has the Reformation taken root in England and among the northern nations of Europe while in Spain and Italy it has left scarcely a trace? Why does the Holy Spirit blow here and not there? Is it not that He does as He wills? "I will have mercy on whom I will have mercy, and I will have compassion on whom I will have compassion" (Rom. 9:15) is the declaration of the divine sovereignty, and the Spirit of God in His movements confirms it.

Among the nations where the Spirit of God is at work, how is it that He blesses one man and not another? How is it that, of two men hearing the same sermon and subject to the same influences at home, one is taken and the other left? Two children nursed at the same breast and trained by the same parents grow up to different ends. He who perishes in sin has no one to blame but himself, but he who is saved ascribes it all to grace—why did that grace come to him? We never dare to lay the fault of man's not repenting and believing upon God; that rests with the evil will which refused to obey the Gospel. However, we dare not ascribe the saving difference in the case of the one who believes to any natural goodness in himself, but we attribute it all to the grace of God and believe that the Holy Spirit works in such "to will and to do of his good pleasure" (Phil. 2:13). But why does He work in us or in any of the chosen? Ah, why? "The wind bloweth where it listeth" (John 3:8).

So, too, is it with the blessing which rests upon ministries. One man wins souls to God and, as a joyous reaper, returns with full sheaves, but another who goes forth with strong desires and seems at least to be as earnest as his fellow comes home with a scanty handful of ears which he has painfully gleaned. Why is one man's net full of fish and another's utterly empty? One servant of the Lord seems, whenever he stands up to preach the Gospel, to attract men to Jesus as though he had golden chains in his mouth which he did cast about men's hearts to draw them in joyful captivity to his Lord, while another cries in bitterness of soul, "Who hath believed our report?" (Isa. 53:1). Truly, "the wind bloweth where it listeth" (John 3:8).

Yes, and these changes happen to each man separately. One day the preacher will be all alive. His spirit will be stirred within him, and he will speak evidently with the Holy Spirit sent down from heaven. Tomorrow, he will find himself dull and heavy even to his own consciousness and even more so to his people's experience, for the power rests not upon him. One day he speaks like the voice of God, and another day he is like a reed shaken by the wind. His fat cattle of years gone by are devoured by the lean cattle of the present. He has his famine as well as his plenty. You will see him come forth today with the unction of the Lord upon him and his face shining with the glory of fellowship with the Most High, and tomorrow he will say, "Look not upon me, for I am black with sin," for the glory will have departed.

We know what it is to come forth like Samson when his locks were shorn and to shake ourselves as at other times and discover that the Lord is not with us. Why all this? Is it not because "the wind bloweth where it listeth" (John 3:8)? The Holy Spirit, for His own wise reasons, puts not forth an equal power upon any man at all times. We cannot control nor command the Spirit of the living God; He is in the highest sense a free agent. "Thy free spirit" (Ps. 51:12) is a name which David gave Him, and a most appropriate name it is.

The wind too has, at least in some lands, its times and seasons. We know that at certain times of the year we may expect winds, and even if they do not come a day or two, as a rule, the month is stormy. There are also trade winds and monsoons which blow with remarkable regularity and are counted upon by mariners.

So it is with the Spirit of God. We know that at certain times He visits the churches and under certain conditions puts forth His power. If, for instance, there is mighty prayer, you may be sure the Spirit of God is at work. If the people of God meet together and besiege the throne of grace with cries and tears, the spiritual barometer indicates that the blessed wind is rising.

Besides, the Holy Spirit has graciously connected Himself with two things: truth and prayer. Preach the truth, publish the Gospel of Jesus Christ, and it is the habit of the Holy Spirit to make the Word quick and powerful to the hearts of men. If we falsify His Word, if we keep back part of the truth, if we become unfaithful, we cannot expect the Holy Spirit to bless us; however, if our teaching is Christ crucified, lovingly set forth, and if the grace of God in its fullness is really declared, the Holy Spirit will attend the truth and make it the great power of God. I will not say that it is always and without exception so, but I think exceptions must be rare. Almost invariably the Spirit bears witness with the truth in the conversion of men.

So too with prayer; the Holy Spirit is pleased to connect Himself with that also, if it is believing prayer. Here the connection is exceedingly intimate because it is the Spirit of God who Himself gives the believing prayer. It is not only true that the Spirit will be given in answer to prayer, but the Spirit is already given or the believing prayer would never have been offered. The spirit of prayerfulness, the spirit of anxiety for the conversion of men, is one of the surest indications that the Holy Spirit is already at work in the minds of His people.

Coming back, however, to the great fact that we cannot command the Holy Spirit, what influence ought that truth to have upon us? Should it not be just this: it should lead us to be very tender and jealous in our conduct towards the Holy Spirit so that we do not grieve Him and cause Him to depart from us. Vex not the Spirit. When you enjoy His gracious operations, be devoutly grateful and walk humbly before God that you may retain them. When He is at work, let not negligence on your part cause you to receive the grace of God in vain.

The wind blew, but the sailor was asleep. It was a favorable breeze, but he had cast anchor. Therefore, his ship moved not. If he had but known it, all through the night he would have spread his sail and would have made good headway towards his port. But he slumbered, and the blessed wind whistled through the ropes, and the ship lay idle at its moorings. Let it not be so with us. Never suffer the Spirit of

God to be with us and find us unmindful of His presence.

In the olden times, when country people depended on the use of the windmill to grind their corn, some parishes would be half-starved when week after week there had been no wind. The miller would look up anxiously, and everybody in the parish would become a watchman for his sails, hoping that they would soon be set in motion. If the breeze stirred in the dead of night and the miller was sound asleep, somebody would run and wake him up. "The wind is blowing, the wind is blowing, grind our corn." So it ought to be whenever the Spirit of God is vigorously working in His church; we should eagerly avail ourselves of His power. We should be so anxious for His divine operations that all should be on the watch so that if some did not discover it, others would, and observant ones would cry, "The Holy Spirit is working with us; let us arise and labor more abundantly." Hoist sail when the wind favors. You cannot command it; therefore, carefully value it.

But we must pass on. The Holy Spirit is described as being like the wind as to His manifestations. "Thou hearest," says Jesus, "the sound thereof" (John 3:8). It has been suggested, and some have enlarged upon it,

that there are many other manifestations of
the presence of wind. You can feel it, you can
see its results upon the trees and the waves,
and sometimes you can be sure that the wind
has been at work by the devastation which it
has caused. However, in this place our Savior
was not so much alluding to a great wind as to
the gentler breezes. The Greek word *pneuma*
is translated "breath" and can hardly be made
to mean a tempest. It was a gentle wind like a
zephyr of which the Lord was speaking here.

The great winds, as I have already said,
can be somewhat calculated upon, but if you sit
in the garden in the cool of the evening, it is
utterly impossible for you to tell from where
the zephyrs come and where they go. They are
so volatile in their movements and untrackable
in their course; here, there, everywhere the
soft breezes of evening steal among the flowers. Our Lord tells us that such gentle zephyrs
are heard. Nicodemus, in the stillness of the
night, could hear them. "Thou hearest the
sound thereof" (John 3:8). The leaves rustle,
and that is all. You hear a gentle movement of
branch and stem as if it were the tinkling of
flowerbells, and so you discover that the wind
is flitting among the beds and borders.

Now, beloved, this shows us that the hearing ear is intended by God to be the discerner of

the Spirit to men, to most men the only discerner that they have. "Thou hearest the sound thereof" (John 3:8). What a wonderful dignity the Lord has been pleased to put upon this little organ, the ear. The Roman church always gives the preference to the eye; its priests are always for astonishing men into grace with their wonderful performances. But, God's way is "faith cometh by hearing" (Rom. 10:17), and the first detector of the Holy Spirit is the ear. To some men this is the only revealer of His mysterious presence, as I have already said; they hear the sound thereof, that is to say, they hear the Gospel preached and hear the word of God read.

Truth, when it is couched in words, is the rustling of the Holy Wind; it is the footstep of the Eternal Spirit as He mysteriously passes along a congregation. Oh, what grief it is that some never get any further than this but abide where Nicodemus was at the first; they hear the sound thereof and nothing more. Some of you are now daily hearing truth which has saved thousands, but it does not save you. You are hearing the very truth which peoples heaven, but yet it leaves you without a hope of eternal life. Yet be sure of this, "the kingdom of God is come nigh unto you" (Luke 10:9, 11). "Thou hearest the sound thereof" (John 3:8), and that wind whose whispers you hear is not far from your own cheek. When you hear the rustling among the boughs of the trees, the breezes are not far to seek, nor is the Spirit of God far away when His sound is heard.

Some hearers, however, go further, for they hear the sound of the Spirit in their consciences, and it disturbs them. They would sleep as others do, but the wind sometimes comes whistling through the keyhole or howls down the chimney and wakes the sluggard. Or, if the man is lying in a garden asleep, the breezes play around his ears and face and startle him. So is it with many unconverted people. They cannot be quiet, for they hear the sound of the Holy Spirit in their consciences and are troubled and perplexed. There is a revival, and they are not saved. However, they are startled and alarmed by it. Their sisters are converted; they are not. Still, it comes very near them, and they feel as if arrows had gone whizzing by their own ears. It is hard living in a careless state in the midst of revival. "Thou hearest the sound thereof" (John 3:8).

Some of you are hearing the sound in your consciences now that in your family circle one after another of your relatives has been brought to know the Lord. You cannot avoid feeling that there is something powerful abroad, though it has not yet exerted its regenerating power upon you.

As for the man who is saved, he hears the Holy Spirit in the most emphatic sense, and with what variety that sound comes to him. At first he heard it as a threatening wind which bowed him in sadness and seemed to sweep all his hopes to the ground as the dry leaves of the forest are carried in the autumn's wind. When the Spirit's voice sounded in my ears at first, it was as a wail of woe, as a wind among the tombs, as a sigh among faded lilies. It seemed as if all my hopes were puffed away like smoke or as the night mists in the morning breeze. Nothing was left me but to mourn my nothingness. Then I heard a sound as of the hot sirocco of the East, as if it issued from a burning oven. You know the text, "The grass withereth, the flower fadeth: because the spirit of the LORD bloweth upon it: surely the people is grass" (Isa. 40:7).

In my soul there had bloomed a fair meadow of golden kingcups and fair flowers of many dainty colors, but the Spirit of God blew thereon and withered it all and left it as a dry, brown, rusty plain on which was neither life nor comeliness. So far the sacred wind destroys that which is evil, but it does not end there, for we thank God we have heard the sound of the

Spirit as a quickening wind. The prophet cried, "Come from the four winds, O breath, and breathe upon these slain, that they may live" (Ezek. 37:9); the wind came, and the dead arose "an exceeding great army" (Ezek. 37:10).

A similar miracle has been wrought on us. The dry bones of our own death have crept together, bone unto His bone, and flesh has come upon them. And now, because of the divine breath, we have begun to live. Now, also, when the Holy Spirit visits us, He renews our life and energy, and we have life more abundantly. The Holy Spirit has since then been to us often like a melting wind: "He causeth his wind to blow, and the waters flow" (Ps. 147:18).

Locked up in the chains of ice all through the winter the waters are still as a stone; however, the spring winds come, the brooklets find liberty and leap away to the rivers, and the rivers flow in all their free force to add their volume to the sea. So has the Spirit of God oftentimes broken up our frost and given our spirits joyous liberty. He melts the rocky heart and dissolves the iron spirit; at the sound of His goings, men are moved to feeling.

We know the sound of this wind as a diffusive breath, drawing forth and diffusing our slumbering graces. "Awake, O north wind; and come, thou south; blow upon my garden, that the spices thereof may flow out" (Song 4:16). Oh, what a sweet unloosing of holy gratitude and love and hope and joy has there been in our hearts when the Spirit of God has visited us. As sweet essences lie hidden in the flowers and come not forth until the loving wind does entice them to fly abroad, so do sweet graces lie within renewed spirits until the Holy Spirit comes and speaks to them. They know His voice and come forth to meet Him, and so sweet fragrances are shed abroad.

Yes, my fellow believers, all this we know, and we have heard the sound of the Holy Spirit in another sense, namely, as going forth with us to the battle of the Lord. We have heard that "sound of a going in the tops of the mulberry trees" (2 Sam. 5:24) which David heard; we have stirred ourselves, and victory has been ours. If we have not heard that rushing mighty wind which came at Pentecost, we still have felt its divine effect which ceases not but still brings life, power, energy, and all that is wanted for the conversion of the sons of men to us who are bidden to go forth and preach the Gospel among the nations. In all these respects the Holy Spirit has manifested Himself, as wind does, by His sound. "Thou hearest the sound thereof" (John 3:8). "Their sound went into all the earth, and their words unto the ends of the world" (Rom. 10:18).

A third likeness of the Spirit to the wind is set before us in the point of mystery. You "canst not tell whence it cometh, and whither it goeth" (John 3:8). Of the wind we may tell that it comes from such and such a quarter or point, but you cannot put your finger on the map and say, "The north wind began in this region," or, "Here the west wind was born." Indeed, we know very little about the winds, their origin, or their laws.

One of the best and most accurate observers of the wind recorded every wind in his region for thirty years. At the end of the term he abandoned the few rules which he had laid down during the first two or three years, for he found that no rule held good. No man can say from where the wind leaps forth. The heathen dreamed of a certain cave wherein the winds were enclosed as in a prison and were allowed to go abroad one by one; it was but a fable. We know not where the winds first spread their wings or where they sleep when all is still. So is it with the Holy Spirit in the mind of man; His first movements are hidden in mystery.

You know that you are converted, my dear friend, you know somewhere about the time, and probably you remember somewhat as to

the means which the Lord used for your salvation. Those outward circumstances you do
know, but how the Holy Spirit operated upon
you, you do not and cannot tell any more than
you can tell how the life swells within the seed
until it springs up and becomes the full corn in
the ear or how the sap in the trees first descends in the winter and afterwards climbs
again in the spring. There are secrets which
nature does not reveal, and the work of the
Spirit is even more a secret. Assuredly, no man
can explain it to his fellow or to himself. Why
is it, my friend, that you obtained a blessing
under one sermon but not under another, and
yet, when you spoke to your sister, she had
been more blessed under the second than the
first? The power does not come from the
preacher, then, it is clear, and you "canst not
tell whence it cometh" (John 3:8).

There are times in which you feel not only
that you can pray but that you must pray. How
do you come to be in that state? I know what it
is to feel in a very ecstasy of delight in the Lord
for which I can scarcely account. At another
time when I have been engaged in the same
work and I think with the same earnestness, I
have not been conscious of any such exceeding
delight in God. At one time the heart will be
full of penitence as if it would break for sin,

and at another season it will overflow with such delight in Christ that the sin seems almost forgotten in the pardoning sacrifice. Why do these diverse operations happen?

We know what it is at times to feel such a sense of death upon us as to be earnestly preparing for our last hours and at another time to be altogether forgetful of death and to be living, as it were, the immortal life already, raised up and sitting together with Christ. But who among us will tell how these various modes and forms and workings of the Spirit come? Go trace the dewdrops, if you can, to the womb of the morning, and discover which way the lightning's flash went or how the thunder rolled along the mountaintops. But you cannot tell nor can you guess from where the Spirit of God comes into your souls.

Nor can we tell where it goes. Here, again, is another mystery. Oh, it charms me to think that when we let loose the truth in the power of the Spirit, we never know where it will fly. A child takes a seed, one of those downy seeds which has its own parachute to bear it through the air. The little one blows it into the air, but who knows where that downy seed will settle and in whose garden it will grow? Such is truth, even from the mouths of babes and sucklings. Whole continents have been covered with strange flowers simply by the wind wafting foreign seeds toward there, and mariners have discovered sunny islands out in the South Seas, where the foot of man has never trodden, covered with abundance of vegetation which the wind has by degrees wafted there. Scatter the truth on all sides, for you cannot tell where the Spirit will carry it. Fling it to the winds, and you will find it after many days. Scatter the living seed with both hands; send it north, south, east, and west, and God will give it wings.

> Waft, waft ye winds the story,
>   And you, ye waters roll,
> Till like a sea of glory
>   It spreads from pole to pole.

I received a letter but the other day when I was sorely sick. It was written by a sister in Christ in the very heart of the empire of Brazil. She said that she had read a copy of my *Morning Readings* and had found thereby the way of peace; therefore, she wrote me such a loving, touching letter that, as I read it, it brought tears to my eyes. There was something more affecting yet: at the end was written in another hand some words to the effect that his dear wife who had written the above letter had died soon after finishing it, and with a bleeding heart the lone husband was sending it on to me, rejoicing that ever the Word came to his wife's soul in the far-off land.

Fellow believers, you do not know where the Word will go and the Spirit with it. In Bohemia, the papists thought they had stamped out the Gospel, and with cruel edicts they kept down all thought of Protestantism. Just lately, however, since the toleration, the Gospel has been preached in that country. To the surprise of everybody there, men and women have come forward from lone cottages in the woods and from different corners of the great cities of Bohemia, bringing with them ancient copies of the Word of God, themselves being eager to know the precious truth for which they remember that their fathers died. A truth will go down the centuries; like the river, it sings,

> Men may come and men may go,
>   But I go on forever.

You "canst not tell...whither it goeth" (John 3:8); it will travel on until the millennium. Send that saying—that the truth cannot die—abroad. The persecutor cannot kill it; it is immortal, like the God who sent it forth. The persecutor cannot even stay its course; it is divine. Popery will always be in danger so long as there is one leaf of the Bible upon earth or one man living who knows the Savior. Antichrist cannot triumph; the Holy Spirit wars against it with the sword of the Word, and you cannot tell how far into the heart of error any truth may be driven. To the overthrow of falsehood and the death of sin, the Spirit speeds on, but you know not how.

You "canst not tell...whither it goeth" (John 3:8) either in any one heart. If you have received the Holy Spirit into your heart, you cannot tell where He will carry you. I am sure that William Carey, when he gave his young heart to Christ, never thought the Spirit of God would carry him to Serampore to preach the Gospel to the Hindus. When George Whitefield first drank of the life-giving Spirit, it never occurred to him that the waiter at the Bell Inn at Gloucester would thunder the Gospel over two continents and turn thousands to Christ. No!

You know not to what blessed end this wind will waft you. Commit yourselves to it; do not be disobedient to the heavenly vision. Be ready to be born along since the Spirit of God will carry you like the dust in the summer's breeze. And, child of God, you do not know yourself to what heights of holiness and degrees of knowledge and ecstasies of enjoyment the Spirit of God will bear you.

"Eye hath not seen, nor ear heard...the things which God hath prepared for them that love him" (1 Cor. 2:9), and though He has revealed them by His Spirit, "for the Spirit searcheth all things, yea, the deep things of God" (1 Cor. 2:10), yet even to the best taught child of God it is not yet fully known where the Spirit of God goes. "Trust ye in the LORD for ever: for in the LORD JEHOVAH is everlasting strength" (Isa. 26:4), and He will bear you onward and upward, even to perfection itself. And you will be with Jesus where He is and behold His glory.

Those Who Are Born of the Spirit

"The wind bloweth where it listeth, and thou hearest the sound thereof, but canst not tell whence it cometh, and whither it goeth: so is every one that is born of the Spirit" (John 3:8). The newborn partakes of the natures of the parent. That which is born of the Spirit is like unto the Spirit of which it is born, even as that which is born of the flesh is flesh and is similar to the flesh by which it is begotten. The twice-born man is like the Holy Spirit who produced him, and he is like Him in each of the points which we have already dwelled upon.

As to freedom, you may say of Him, "He blows where He pleases." The Spirit of God makes the believer a free man, bestows on him the freedom of His will which he never had before, and gives him a delightful consciousness of liberty. "If the Son therefore shall make you free, ye shall be free indeed" (John 8:36). I do not affirm that every spiritual man does what pleases the Spirit because, alas, I see another law in our members warring against the law of our mind and "bringing [us] into captivity to the law of sin [and death]" (Rom. 7:23). But still, "where the Spirit of the Lord is, there is liberty" (2 Cor. 3:17).

Now you can pray, which you could not do before. Now you can praise, though you could not extract a note of praise from your ungrateful heart before. Now you can cry, "Abba, Father" (Rom. 8:15). Now you can draw near to God. You are no longer under man's control; you blow where you will. You are not now ruled by priestly crafts or domineered over by the opinion of your fellowman. The Lord has set you free, and you want to go where God's Word bids you go and find the utmost liberty in going that way. Oh, fellow believers, I cannot tell you the change which is felt by a regenerate man in the matter of spiritual liberty. When you were under the bondage of the law, of custom, of sin, and of fear of death and dread of hell, you were like a man shut up in one of those cells in Venice which lies below the level of the water mark, where the air is foul and the poor prisoner can only stir a half dozen feet and then walk back again in the darkness. But when the Spirit of God comes, He brings the soul from darkness into light, from clammy damp into the open air. He sets before you an open door; He helps you to run in the way of God's commands; and as if that were not enough, He even lends you wings and bids you mount as the eagle, for He has set you free.

Again, the man who is born of the Spirit is somewhat manifested and is known by his sound. "Thou hearest the sound thereof" (John 3:8). The most ungodly man, if he lives near a Christian, will hear the sound of him. The secret life within will speak. Words there will be, for Christians are not dumb, but actions will speak more loudly still. Even apart from actions, the very spirit and tone of the man who is really regenerated will speak, and the ungodly man will be compelled to hear it. "Thou hearest the sound thereof" (John 3:8).

Now, notice the mystery there is about a Christian. You know nothing, if you are unregenerate, about the life the believer leads, for he is dead and his life "is hid with Christ in God" (Col. 3:3). You know not from where he comes forth in the morning. Those beds of spices which have made his garments fragrant you have not seen. That weeping in prayer or that rejoicing in fellowship with which he began the morning you know nothing of, and you cannot know until you are born of the Spirit yourself. Nor can you tell where the spiritual man goes. In the midst of his trouble you see him calm; do you know where he went to win that rare quietude? In the hour of death you see him triumphant; do you know where he has been to learn to die so joyously? No, the unregenerate man knows not where the believer goes. There is a secret place of the Most High, and they who have once learned to enter under "the shadow of the Almighty" (Ps. 91:1) will abide there. Carnal men, though, will not come into this secret chamber.

The Christian life is a mystery all the way through from its beginning to its end—to the world all a mystery and to the Christian himself a puzzle. He cannot read his own riddle or understand himself. This one thing he knows: "Whereas I was blind, now I see" (John 9:25). This also he knows: "O LORD, truly I am thy servant; I am thy servant, and the son of thine handmaid: thou hast loosed my bonds" (Ps. 116:16). This also he knows, that when his Lord will be revealed, then will he also shine forth as the sun. The life within him in its coming and going is all a mystery to him, but he blesses God that he has fellowship therein. He goes on his way feeling that, though men know not where he is or where he is going, yet the Lord knows him. He himself is sure that he is going to his Father and his God.

Oh, that every one of you had so delightful a hope. The Lord grant it to you, for Jesus' sake.

Chapter 4

The Pentecostal Wind and Fire

And suddenly there came a sound from heaven as of a rushing mighty wind, and it filled all the house where they were sitting. And there appeared unto them cloven tongues like as of fire, and it sat upon each of them. And they were all filled with the Holy Ghost, and began to speak with other tongues, as the Spirit gave them utterance.
—Acts 2:2–4

From the descent of the Holy Spirit at the beginning, we may learn something concerning His operations at the present time. Remember at the outset that whatever the Holy Spirit was at the first, He is now; as God, He remains forever the same. Whatever He then did, He is able to do still, for His power is by no means diminished. As the prophet Micah says, "O thou that art named the house of Jacob, is the spirit of the LORD straitened?" (Mic. 2:7). We should greatly grieve the Holy Spirit if we supposed that His might was less today than in the beginning. Although we may not expect, and need not desire, the miracles which came with the gift of the Holy Spirit, so far as they were physical, we may both desire and expect that which was intended and symbolized by them. We may reckon to see similar spiritual wonders performed among us at this time.

Pentecost, according to the belief of the Jews, was the time of the giving of the law; therefore, if there was a marvelous display of power on Sinai when the law was given, it was to be expected that when the Gospel was given, whose assistance is far more glorious, there should be some special unveiling of the divine presence. If, at the commencement of the Gospel, we behold the Holy Spirit working great signs and wonders, may we not expect a continuance—if anything, an increased display—of His power as the ages roll on? The law vanished away, but the Gospel will never vanish. It shines more and more to the perfect millennial day. Therefore, I reckon that, with the sole exception of physical miracles, whatever was wrought by the Holy Spirit at the first we may look to be wrought continually while the dispensation lasts.

It ought not to be forgotten that Pentecost was the feast of first fruits; it was the time when the first ears of ripe corn were offered to God. If, then, at the commencement of the gospel harvest we see so plainly the power of the Holy Spirit, may we not most properly expect infinitely more as the harvest advances and most of all when the most numerous sheaves will be gathered in? May we not conclude that if the Pentecost was so marvelous, the actual harvest will be more wonderful still?

My object is not to talk of the descent of the Holy Spirit as a piece of history but to view it as a fact bearing upon us at this hour, even upon us who are called in these latter days to bear our testimony for the truth. The Father has sent us the Comforter that He may dwell in us until the coming of the Lord. The Holy Spirit has never returned to the Father, for He came to abide with us forever, in accordance with the Savior's prayer. The gift of the Comforter was not temporary, and the display of His power was not to be seen just once and no more.

The Holy Spirit is here, and we ought to respect His divine working among us. If He does not so work, we should search ourselves to see what it is that hinders and whether there may not be something in ourselves which vexes Him so that He restrains His sacred energy and does not work among us as He did before.

May God grant that this meditation may increase our faith in the Holy Spirit and inflame our desires towards Him so that we may look to see Him fulfilling His mission among men as at the beginning.

The Instructive Symbols of the Holy Spirit

There were two such symbols that were made prominent at Pentecost. There was a sound "as of a rushing mighty wind" (Acts 2:2), and there were "cloven tongues like as of fire" (Acts 2:3).

Take the symbols separately. The first is wind—an emblem of Deity and therefore a proper symbol of the Holy Spirit. Often in the Old Testament, God revealed Himself under the emblem of breath or wind; indeed, as most of you know, the Hebrew word for "wind" and "spirit" is the same. The Greek word is the same; when Christ talked to Nicodemus, it is not very easy for translators to tell us when He said "spirit" and when He said "wind." Indeed, some most correctly render the original all the way through by the word "wind," while others with much reason have also used the word "spirit" in their translations. The original word signified either the one or the other or both.

Wind is, of all material things, one of the most spiritual in appearance. It is invisible, ethereal, mysterious; hence, men have fixed upon it as being the most nearly akin to spirit. In Ezekiel's famous vision, when he saw the valley full of dry bones, we all know that the Spirit of God was intended by that vivifying wind which came when the prophet prophesied and blew upon the withered relics until they were quickened into life. "The LORD hath his way in the whirlwind" (Nah. 1:3), thus He displays Himself when He works. "The LORD answered Job out of the whirlwind" (Job 38:1), thus He reveals Himself when He teaches His servants.

Observe that this wind on the day of Pentecost was accompanied with a sound—a sound "as of a rushing mighty wind" (Acts 2:2)—for although the Spirit of God can work in silence, in saving operations He frequently uses sound. I would be the last to depreciate meetings in which there is nothing but holy silence, for I could wish that we had more reverence for silence, and it is in stillness that the inner life is nourished. However, the Holy Spirit does not work for the advancement of the kingdom of God by silence alone, for "faith cometh by hearing" (Rom. 10:17).

There is a sound "as of a rushing mighty wind" (Acts 2:2) when the Word is sounded forth throughout whole nations by the publishing of the Gospel. The sound came on this occasion, no doubt, to call the attention of the assembly to what was about to occur, to arouse them, and to fill them with awe. There is something indescribably solemn about the rush of a rising tempest; it bows the soul before the sublime mystery of divine power. What more fitting as an attendant upon divine working than the deeply solemn rush of a mighty wind.

With this awe-inspiring sound as of a mighty wind, there was clear indication of its coming from heaven. Ordinary winds blow from this or that quarter of the skies, but this descended from heaven itself. It was distinctly like a downdraft from above. This sets forth the fact that the true Spirit, the Spirit of God, neither comes from this place, nor can His power be controlled or directed by human authority. But His working is ever from above, from God Himself. The work of the Holy Spirit is, so to speak, the breath of God, and His power is evermore in a special sense the immediate power of God. Coming downward, therefore, this mysterious wind passed into the chamber where the disciples were assembled and filled the room. An ordinary, rushing, mighty wind would have been felt outside the room and would probably have destroyed the house or injured the inmates if it had been aimed at any one building. However, this heavenly gust filled but did not destroy the room; it blessed but did not overthrow the waiting company.

The meaning of the symbol is that as breath, air, or wind is the very life of man, so is the Spirit of God the life of the spiritual man. By Him are we quickened at the first; by Him are we kept alive afterwards; by Him is the inner life nurtured and increased and perfected. The breath of the nostrils of the man of God is the Spirit of God.

This holy breath was not only intended to quicken them but to invigorate them. They took in great draughts of heavenly life; they felt animated, aroused, and stirred. A sacred enthusiasm came upon them because they were filled with the Holy Spirit, and, girded with that strength, they rose into a nobler form of life than they had known before.

No doubt this wind was intended to show the irresistible power of the Holy Spirit. Simple as the air is, and mobile and apparently feeble, set it in motion, and you feel that a thing of life is among you. Make that motion more rapid, and who knows the power of the restless giant that has been awakened. See, it becomes a storm, a tempest, a hurricane, a tornado, a cyclone. Nothing can be more potent than the wind when it is thoroughly roused. Yet, though the Spirit of God is despised among men so much that they do not even believe in His existence, let Him work with the fullness of His power, and you will see what He can do.

He comes softly, breathing like a gentle zephyr which fans the flowers but does not dislodge the insect of most gauzy wing, and our hearts are comforted. He comes like a stirring breeze, and we are quickened to a livelier diligence. Our sails are hoisted, and we fly before the gale. He comes with yet greater strength, and we prostrate ourselves in the dust as we hear the thunder of His power bringing down with a crash false confidences and refuges of lies. How the firm reliances of carnal men, which seemed to stand like rocks, are utterly cast down! How men's hopes, which appeared to be rooted like oaks, are torn up by the roots before the breath of the convincing Spirit. What can stand against Him? Oh, that we may but see in these latter days something of that mighty, rushing wind which breaks the cedars of Lebanon and sweeps before it all things that would resist its power.

The second Pentecostal symbol was fire. Fire again is a frequent symbol of the Deity.

Abraham saw a burning lamp, and Moses beheld a burning bush. When Solomon had built his holy and beautiful house, its consecration lay in the fire of God descending upon the sacrifice to mark that the Lord was there. When the Lord had dwelled before then in the tabernacle, which was superseded by the temple, He revealed Himself in a pillar of cloud by day and a pillar of fire by night. (See Exodus 13:21.) "Our God is a consuming fire" (Heb. 12:29). Hence, the symbol of fire is a fit emblem of God the Holy Spirit. Let us adore and worship Him.

Tongues of flame sitting on each man's head were tokens of a personal visitation to the mind and heart of each one of the chosen company. The fires came not to consume them, for no one was injured by the flaming tongue. To men whom the Lord has prepared for His approach, there is no danger in His visitations. They see God, and their lives are preserved. They feel His fires and are not consumed. This is the privilege of those alone who have been prepared and purified for such fellowship with God.

The intention of the symbol was to show them that the Holy Spirit would illuminate them as fire gives light. "He will guide you into all truth" (John 16:13). Henceforth, they were to be no longer untrained children but to be teachers in Israel, instructors of the nations whom they were to disciple unto Christ. Hence, the Spirit of light was upon them. But fire does more than give light; it inflames, and the flames which sat upon each showed them that they were to be ablaze with love, intense with zeal, burning with self-sacrifice.

These flames also showed them that they were to go forth among men to speak not with the chilling tongues of deliberate logic but with burning tongues of passionate pleading, persuading and entreating men to come to Christ that they might live. The fire signified inspiration. God was about to make them speak under a divine influence, to speak "as the Spirit gave them utterance" (Acts 2:4). Oh, blessed symbol, I pray to God that all of us would experience its meaning to the full and that the tongue of fire would sit upon every servant of the Lord. May a fire burn steadily within to destroy our sin, a holy, sacrificial flame to make us whole burnt offerings unto God, a never-dying flame of zeal for Him and devotion to the Cross.

Note that the emblem was not only fire but a tongue of fire. God meant to have a speaking church, not a church that would fight with the sword—we have nothing to do with that weapon—but a church that would have a sword proceeding out of its mouth, whose one weapon should be the proclamation of the Gospel of Jesus Christ. I think from what I know of some preachers that when they had their Pentecost, the influence sat upon them in the form of tongues of flowers, but the apostolic Pentecost knew not flowers but flames. What fine preaching we have nowadays! What new thoughts and poetical turns! This is not the style of the Holy Spirit. Soft and gentle is the flow of smooth speech which tells of the dignity of man, the grandeur of the century, the toning down of all punishment for sin, and the probable restoration of all lost spirits, including the archfiend himself. This is the satanic ministry, subtle as the serpent and as his seducing words to Eve.

The Holy Spirit does not call us to this mode of speech. Show fire, intensity, zeal, passion as much as you will, but aiming at effect by polished phrases and brilliant periods is more fit for those who would deceive men than for those who would tell them the message of the Most High. The style of the Holy Spirit is one which conveys the truth to the mind in the most forcible manner; it is plain but flaming, simple but consuming. The Holy Spirit has never written a cold period throughout the whole Bible, and never did

He speak by a man a lifeless word. Evermore, He gives and blesses the tongue of fire.

These, then, are the two symbols: He comes as the wind which wafts the words we speak and as fire which burns a way for the truth we utter. Our words are now full of life and flame. They are born by the breath of the Spirit, and they fall like flames and set the souls of men blazing with desire after God. If the Holy Spirit will rest upon me or upon you, or upon any of us, to qualify us for service, it will be after this fashion: not merely of life for ourselves but of fiery energy in dealing with others. Come on us even now, rushing, mighty wind and tongue of fire, for the world has great need. It lies stagnant in the malaria of sin and needs a healing wind. It is shrouded in dreadful night and needs the flaming torch of truth. There is neither health nor light for it but from You, blessed Spirit. Come, then, upon it through Your people.

Now, put these two symbols together; only mind what you are doing. Wind and fire together! I have kept them separate in my discourse previously, and you have seen power in each one. What are they together? Rushing, mighty wind alone, how terrible! Who will stand against it? See how the gallant ships dash together and the monarchs of the forest bow their heads. And fire alone! Who will stand against it when it devours its prey? But set wind and fire to work in hearty union! Remember the old city of London. When first the flames began, it was utterly impossible to quench them because the wind fanned the flame and the buildings gave way before the fire torrent.

Oh, God, send us the Holy Spirit in this fashion; give us both the breath of spiritual life and the fire of unconquerable zeal until nation after nation will yield to the sway of Jesus. Oh, You who are our God, answer us by fire, we pray You. Answer us both by wind and fire, and then will we see You to be God indeed. The kingdom comes not, and the work is flagging. Oh, that You would send the wind and the fire! You will do this when we are all of one accord, all believing, all expecting, all prepared by prayer. Lord, bring us to this waiting state.

The Immediate Effects of the Descent of the Holy Spirit

Because these symbols were not sent in vain, there were two immediate effects: the first was filling, and the second was the gift of utterance. I call special attention to the first, namely, filling. "It filled all the house where they were sitting" (Acts 2:2), and it did not merely fill the house but the man: "They were all filled with the Holy Ghost" (Acts 2:4). When they stood up to speak, even the ribald mockers in the crowd noticed this, for they said, "These men are full," and though they added "of new wine" (Acts 2:13), they evidently detected a singular fullness about them. We are poor, empty things by nature and useless while we remain so. We need to be filled with the Holy Spirit.

Where the Spirit of God is truly at work, He first fills and then gives utterance; that is His way. Oh, that you and I were at this moment filled with the Holy Spirit. "Full." Then they were not cold and dead and empty of life as we sometimes are. "Full." Then there was no room for anything else in any one of them! They were too completely occupied by the heavenly power to have room for the desires of the flesh. Fear was banished, every minor motive was expelled, and the Spirit of God, as He flooded their very beings, drove out of them everything that was extraneous. They had many faults and many infirmities before, but that day, when they were filled with the Spirit of God, faults and infirmities were no more perceptible. They became different men from what they had ever been before; men full of

God are the reverse of men full of self. Out of a full church, the world will receive salvation but never out of an empty one. The first thing we want as a church is to be filled with the Holy Spirit; the gift of utterance will then come as a matter of course.

The next Pentecostal symbol was utterance. As soon as the Spirit of God filled them, they began to speak at once. It seems to me that they began to speak before the people had come together. They could not help it; the inner forces demanded expression, and they had to speak. So when the Spirit of God really comes upon a man, he does not wait until he has gathered an audience of the size which he desires, but he seizes the next opportunity. He speaks to one person, he speaks to two, he speaks to three, and he speaks to anybody. He must speak, for he is full and must have vent.

When the Spirit of God fills a man, he speaks so as to be understood. The crowd spoke different languages, and these Spirit-taught men spoke to them in the languages of the countries in which they were born. This is one of the signs of the Spirit's utterance. If my friend over yonder talks in a Latinized style to a company of fruit sellers, I will warrant you the Holy Spirit has nothing to do with him. If a learned brother fires over the heads of his congregation with a grand oration, he may trace his elocution, if he likes, to Cicero and Demosthenes, but do not let him ascribe it to the Holy Spirit, for that is not after His manner. The Spirit of God speaks so that His words may be understood; if there is any obscurity, it lies in the language used by the Lord Himself.

The crowd not only understood, but they felt. There were knives in this Pentecostal preaching, and the hearers "were pricked in their heart" (Acts 2:37). The truth wounded men, and the slain of the Lord were many, for the wounds were in the most vital parts. They could not make it out; they had heard speakers before, but this was quite a different thing. The men spoke flames, and one hearer cried to his fellow, "What is this?" The preachers were speaking flames, and the fire dropped into the hearts of men until they were amazed and confounded.

Those are the two effects of the Holy Spirit: a fullness of the Spirit in the ministry and the church and, next, a fire ministry and a church on fire, speaking so as to be felt and understood by those around. Causes produce effects like themselves, and this wind and fire ministry soon did its work. We read that this "was noised abroad" (Acts 2:6). Of course it was, because there had been a noise "as of a rushing mighty wind" (Acts 2:2). Next to that, we read that all the people came together and were confounded. There was naturally a stir, for a great wind from heaven was rushing. All were amazed and astonished, and while some inquired believingly, others began to mock. Of course, they did. There was a fire burning, and fire is a dividing thing. This fire began to separate between the precious and the vile, as it always will do when it comes into operation. We may expect at the beginning of a true revival to observe a movement, a noise, and a stir among the people. These things are not done in a corner. Cities will know of the presence of God, and crowds will be attracted by the event.

This was the immediate effect of the Pentecostal marvel.

The Most Prominent Subject

Suppose that the Holy Spirit should work mightily in the church; what would our ministers preach about? "We do hear them speak in our own tongues the wonderful works of God" (Acts 2:11). Their subject was the wonderful works of God. Oh, that this might be to my dying day my sole and only topic: "the wonderful works of God." For, first, these full men spoke of redemption, that wonderful work of God. Peter's sermon was a specimen of how they spoke of it. He told the people that Jesus was the Son of God, that they had crucified and slain Him, but that He had come to redeem men and that there was salvation through His precious blood. He preached redemption.

Oh, how this land will echo again and again with, "Redemption, redemption, redemption, redemption by the precious blood," when the Holy Spirit is with us. This is fit fuel for the tongue of flame; this is something worthy to be wafted by the divine wind. "God was in Christ, reconciling the world unto himself, not imputing their trespasses unto them" (2 Cor. 5:19). "The blood of Jesus Christ his Son cleanseth us from all sin" (1 John 1:7). This is one of the wonderful works of God of which we can never make too frequent mention.

They certainly spoke of the next wonderful work of God, namely, regeneration. There was no concealing of the work of the Holy Spirit in that primitive ministry. It was brought to the forefront. Peter said, "Ye shall receive the gift of the Holy Ghost" (Acts 2:38). The preachers of Pentecost told of the Spirit's work by the Spirit's power: conversion, repentance, renewal, faith, holiness, and such things were freely spoken of and ascribed to their real author, the divine Spirit. If the Spirit of God will give us once again a full and fiery ministry, we will hear it clearly proclaimed, "Ye must be born again" (John 3:7), and we will see a people forthcoming who are "born, not of blood, nor of the will of the flesh...but of [the will of] God" (John 1:13) and by the energy which comes from heaven. A Holy Spirit ministry cannot be silent about the Holy Spirit and His sacred operations upon the heart.

Very plainly they spoke of a third wonderful work of God, namely, remission of sins. This was the point that Peter pushed home to them: that on repentance they should receive remission of sins. What a blessed message is this: pardon for crimes of deepest depravity, a pardon bought with Jesus' blood, free pardon, full pardon, irreversible pardon, given to the vilest of the vile when they grind their weapons of rebellion and bow at the feet that once were nailed to the tree. If we would prove ourselves to be under divine influence, we must keep to the divine message of fatherly forgiveness to returning prodigals. What happier word can we deliver?

These are the doctrines which the Holy Spirit will revive in the midst of the land when

He works mightily: redemption, regeneration, remission. If you would have the Spirit of God resting on your labors, dear brothers and sisters, keep these three things ever to the front, and make all men hear in their own tongue "the wonderful works of God" (Acts 2:11).

The Glorious Results

The result of the Spirit coming as wind and fire, filling and giving utterance, was first in the hearers' deep feeling. There was never, perhaps, in the world such a feeling excited by the language of mortal man as that which was aroused in the crowds in Jerusalem on that day. You might have seen a group here and a group there all listening to the same story of the wondrous works of God and all stirred and affected, for the heavenly wind and fire went with the preaching, and they could not help feeling its power. We are told that they were pricked in the heart. They had painful emotions; they felt wounds which killed their enmity. The word struck at the center of a person's being; it pierced the vital point.

Alas, people come into our places of worship nowadays to hear the preacher, and their friends ask them on their return, "How did you like him?" Was that your errand, to see how you liked him? What practical benefit is there in such a mode of using the servants of God? Are we sent among you to give opportunities for criticism? Yet most men seem to think that we are nothing better than fiddlers or actors who come upon the stage to help you while away an hour. Oh, my readers, if we are true to our God, and true to you, ours is a more solemn business than most men dream. The object of all true preaching is the heart; we aim at divorcing the heart from sin and wedding it to Christ. Our ministry has failed and has not the divine seal set upon it unless it makes men tremble, makes them sad, and then presently brings them to Christ and causes them to rejoice.

Then followed an earnest inquiry. "They were pricked in their heart, and said unto Peter and to the rest of the apostles, Men and brethren, what shall we do?" (Acts 2:37). Emotion is of itself but a poor result unless it leads to practical action. To make men feel is well enough, but it must be a feeling which impels them to immediate movement or at least to earnest inquiry as to what they should do.

Oh, Spirit of God, if You will rest on me, even me, men will not hear and go their way and forget what they have heard! They will arise and seek the Father and taste His love. If

You would rest on all the brotherhood that
publishes Your Word, men would not merely
weep while they hear and be affected while the
discouragement lasts, but they would go their
way to ask, "What must [we] do to be saved?"
(Acts 16:30). This is what we need. We do not
require new preachers, but we need a new
anointing of the Spirit. We do not require novel
forms of service, but we want the fire Spirit, the
wind Spirit, to work by us until everywhere
men cry, "What must we do to be saved?"

Then came a grand reception of the
Word. We are told that they gladly received
the Word (Acts 2:41), and they received it in
two senses. First, Peter bade them to repent
(Acts 2:38), and so they did. They were
pricked to the heart from compunction on account of what they had done to Jesus, and
they sorrowed after a godly sort and quit
their sins. They also believed in Him whom
they had slain and accepted Him as their
Savior there and then without hesitating any
longer. They trusted in Him "whom God hath
set forth to be a propitiation" (Rom. 3:25),
and thus they fully received the Word. Repentance and faith make up a complete reception
of Christ, and they had both of these. Why
should we not see this divine result today? We
will see it in proportion to our faith.

But what next? Why, they were baptized directly (Acts 2:41). Having repented and believed, the next step was to make a confession of their faith, and they did not postpone that act for a single day. Why should they? Willing hands were there. The whole company of the faithful were all glad to engage in the holy service, and that same day they were baptized into the name of the Father, the Son, and the Holy Spirit.

If the Holy Spirit were fully with us, we should never have to complain that many believers never confess their faith, for they would be eager to confess the Savior's name in His own appointed way. Backwardness to being baptized comes too often from fear of persecution, indecision, love of ease, pride, or disobedience, but all these vanish when the heavenly wind and fire are doing their sacred work. Sinful diffidence soon disappears, sinful shame of Jesus is no more seen, and hesitancy and delay are banished forever when the Holy Spirit works with power.

Furthermore, there was not merely this immediate confession, but as a result of the Spirit of God there was great steadfastness: "They continued stedfastly in the apostles' doctrine" (Acts 2:42). We have had plenty of revivals of the human sort, and their results have been sadly disappointing. Under excitement, nominal converts have been multiplied, but where are they after a little testing? I am sadly compelled to admit that, so far as I can observe, there has been much sown and very little reaped that was worth reaping from much of that which has been called revival. Our hopes were flattering as a dream, but the apparent result has vanished like a vision of the night. However, where the Spirit of God is really at work, the converts stand. They are well rooted and grounded, and hence they are not "carried about with every wind of doctrine" (Eph. 4:14) but continue steadfast in the apostolic truth.

We see next that there was abundant worship of God, for they were steadfast not only in the doctrine but in breaking of bread and in prayer and in fellowship. There was no difficulty in getting a prayer meeting then, no difficulty in maintaining daily communion then, no want of holy fellowship then, for the Spirit of God was among them and the ordinances were precious in their eyes. "Oh," say some, "if we could get this minister or that evangelist we should do well." Brothers, if you had the Holy Spirit, you would have everything else growing out of His presence, for all good things are summed up in Him.

Next to this, there came striking generosity. Funds were not hard to raise; liberality overflowed its banks as believers poured all that they had into the common fund. Then was it indeed seen to be true that the silver and the gold are the Lord's. When the Spirit of God operates powerfully, there is little need to issue telling appeals for widows and orphans or to go down on your knees and plead for missionary fields which cannot be occupied for want of money. When the Spirit of God comes, those who have substance yield it to their Lord, those who have but little grow rich by giving of that little, and those who are already rich become happy by consecrating what they have. There is no need to rattle the box when the rushing, mighty wind is heard and the fire is dissolving all hearts in love.

Then came continual gladness. They "did eat their meat with gladness" (Acts 2:46). They were not merely glad at prayer meetings and sermons but glad at breakfast and at supper. Whatever they had to eat, they were for singing over it. Jerusalem was the happiest city that ever was when the Spirit of God was there. The disciples were singing from morning to night, and I have no doubt the outsiders asked, "What is it all about?" The temple was never so frequented as then; there was never such singing before; the very streets of Jerusalem and the Hill of Zion rang with the songs of the once despised Galileans.

They were full of gladness, and that gladness showed itself in praising God. I have no doubt they broke out now and then in the services with shouts of "Glory! Hallelujah!" I should not wonder that all propriety was scattered to the winds. They were so glad, so exhilarated, that they were ready to leap for joy. Of course, we never say "Amen" or "Glory" now. We have grown to be so frozenly proper that we never interrupt a service in any way because, to tell the truth, we are not so particularly glad; we are not so specially full of praise that we want to do anything of the sort. Alas, we have lost very much of the Spirit of God and much of the joy and gladness which attend His presence, and so we have settled into a decorous apathy! We gather the pinks of propriety instead of the palm branches of praise.

God, send us a season of glorious disorder. Oh, for a sweep of wind that will set the seas in motion and make our ironclad brothers now lying so quietly at anchor to roll from stem to stern. As for us, who are as the little ships, we will fly before the gale if it will but speed us to our desired haven. Oh, for fire to fall again—fire which will affect the most stolid! This is a sure remedy for indifference. When fire falls into a man's bosom, he knows it, and when the Word of God comes home to a man's soul, he knows it, too. Oh, that such fire might first sit upon the disciples and then fall on all around!

For, to close, there was then a daily increase of the church: "The Lord added to the church daily such as should be saved" (Acts 2:47). Conversion was going on perpetually. Additions to the church were not events which happened once a year, but they were everyday matters. "So mightily grew the word of God and prevailed" (Acts 19:20).

Oh, Spirit of God, You are ready to work with us today even as You did then! Stay not, we beseech You, but work at once. Break down every barrier that hinders the incoming of Your might. Overturn, overturn, sacred wind! Consume all obstacles, heavenly fire, and give us now both hearts of flame and tongues of fire to preach Your reconciling word, for Jesus' sake. Amen.

Chapter 5

The Indwelling and Outflowing of the Spirit

*He that believeth on me, as the scripture hath
said, out of his belly shall flow rivers of living
water. (But this spake he of the Spirit, which
they that believe on him should receive: for the
Holy Ghost was not yet given; because that Jesus
was not yet glorified.)*
—John 7:38–39

*Nevertheless I tell you the truth; It is expedient
for you that I go away: for if I go not away, the
Comforter will not come unto you; but if I depart,
I will send him unto you.*
—John 16:7

I t is essential, dear friends, that we should
worship the living and true God. It will be
ill for us if it can be said, "Ye worship ye
know not what" (John 4:22). "Thou shalt worship the Lord thy God, and him only shalt thou
serve" (Matt. 4:10). The heathen err from this
command by multiplying gods and making this

and that image be the object of their adoration. Their excess runs to gross superstition and idolatry.

I fear that sometimes we who profess and call ourselves Christians err in exactly the opposite direction. Instead of worshipping more than God, I fear we worship less than God. This appears when we forget to pay due adoration to the Holy Spirit of God. The true God is triune: Father, Son, and Holy Spirit. Though there is but one God, that one God has manifested Himself to us in the trinity of His sacred persons. If, then, I worship the Father and the Son but forget or neglect to adore the Holy Spirit, I worship less than God. While the poor heathen in his ignorance goes far beyond and transgresses, I must take care for fear that I too fall short and fail.

What a grievous thing it will be if we do not pay that loving homage and reverence to the Holy Spirit which is so justly His due. May it not be the fact that we enjoy less of His power and see less of His working in the world because the church of God has not been sufficiently mindful of Him? It is a blessed thing to preach the work of Jesus Christ, but it is an evil thing to omit the work of the Holy Spirit, for the work of the Lord Jesus itself is no blessing to that man who does not know the work of the Holy Spirit. There is the ransom price, but it is only through the Spirit that we know the redemption. There is the precious blood, but it is as though the fountain had never been filled unless the Spirit of God leads us with repenting faith to wash therein. The bandage is soft and the ointment is effectual, but the wound will never be healed until the Holy Spirit applies that which the great Physician has provided. Let us not, therefore, be found neglectful of the work of the divine Spirit for fear that we incur guilt and inflict upon ourselves serious damage.

You that are believers have the most forcible reasons to hold the Holy Spirit in the highest esteem, for what are you now without Him? What were you and what would you still have been, if it had not been for His gracious work in you? He quickened you, or else you would not be in the living family of God today. He gave you understanding so that you might know the truth, or else you would have been as ignorant as the carnal world is at this hour. It was He that awakened your conscience, convincing you of sin. It was He that gave you abhorrence of sin and led you to repent. It was He that taught you to believe and made you see that glorious person who is to be believed, even Jesus, the Son of God. The Spirit has wrought in you your faith and love and hope and every grace. There is not a jewel upon the neck of your soul which He did not place there.

> For every virtue we possess,
>   And every victory won,
> And every thought of holiness,
>   Are His alone.

Beloved believers, notwithstanding all that the Spirit of God has already done in us, it is very possible that we have missed a large part of the blessing which He is willing to give, for He "is able to do exceeding abundantly above all that we ask or think" (Eph. 3:20). We have already come to Jesus, and we have drunk of the life-giving stream. Our thirst is quenched, and we are made to live in Him. Is this all? Now that we are living in Him and rejoicing to do so, have we come to the end of the matter? Assuredly not. We have reached as far as that first exhortation of the Master: "If any man thirst, let him come unto me, and drink" (John 7:37). However, do you think that the generality of the church of God has ever advanced to the next verse: "He that believeth on me, as the scripture hath said, out of his belly shall flow rivers of living water" (John 7:38)? I think I am not going beyond the grievous truth if I say that only here and there will you find men and women who have believed up to that point. Their thirst is quenched, as I have said, and they live. Because Jesus lives, they will live also, but health and vigor they do not have. They have life, but they do not have "it more abundantly" (John 10:10). They have little life with which to act upon others. They have no energy welling up and overflowing to go streaming out of them like rivers.

Brothers and sisters, let us go in to get from God all that God will give us. Let us set our hearts upon this, that we mean to have by God's help all that the infinite goodness of God is ready to bestow. Let us not be satisfied with the sip that saves, but let us go on to the baptism which buries the flesh and raises us in the likeness of the risen Lord. Let us seek that baptism into the Holy Spirit and into fire which makes us spiritual and sets us all on flame with zeal for the glory of God and eagerness for usefulness by which that glory may be increased among the sons of men.

Thus I introduce you to my texts, and by their guidance we will enter upon the further consideration of the operations of the Holy Spirit, especially of those to which we would aspire.

The Work of the Spirit Is Intimately Connected with the Work of Christ

It is a great pity when people preach the Holy Spirit's work so as to obscure the work of Christ, and I have known some do that, for they have held up before the sinner's eye the inward experience of believers instead of lifting up first and foremost the crucified Savior to whom we must look and live. The Gospel is not "Behold the Spirit of God" but "Behold the Lamb of God" (John 1:29, 36). It is an equal pity when Christ is so preached that the Holy Spirit is ignored as if faith in Jesus prevented the necessity of the new birth and as if imputed righteousness rendered imparted righteousness needless. Have I not often reminded you that "Except a man be born of water and of the Spirit, he cannot enter into the kingdom of God" (John 3:5)? We also read those blessed words,

And as Moses lifted up the serpent in the wilderness, even so must the Son of man be lifted up: That whosoever believeth in him should not perish, but have eternal life. For God so loved the world, that he gave his only begotten Son, that whosoever believeth in him should not perish, but have everlasting life. (John 3:14–16)

The necessity for regeneration by the Spirit is there put very clearly, and so is the free promise that those who trust in Jesus will be saved. This is what we ought to do: we must take care to let both these truths stand out most distinctly with equal prominence. They are intertwined with each other and are necessary each to each: "What therefore God hath joined together, let not man put asunder" (Matt. 19:6).

They are so joined together that, first of all, the Holy Spirit was not given until Jesus had been glorified. Carefully note our first text; it is a very striking one: "This spake he of the Spirit, which they that believe on him should receive, for the Holy Ghost was not yet" (John 7:39). The word "given" is not in the original. It was inserted by the translators to help make out the meaning. They were perhaps wise in making such an addition, but the words are more forcible by themselves. How strong is the statement, "for the Holy Ghost was not yet." Of course, none of us dream that the Holy Spirit was not yet existing, for He is eternal and self-existent, being most truly God, but He was not yet in fellowship with man to the full extent in which He now is since Jesus Christ is glorified. The near and dear intercourse of God with man which is expressed by the indwelling of the Spirit could not take place until redeeming work was done and the Redeemer was exalted. As far as men were concerned and the fullness of the blessing was concerned, as indicated by the outflowing rivers of living water, the Spirit of God was not yet.

"Oh," say you, "but was not the Spirit of God in the church in the wilderness and with the saints of God in all former ages?" My answer would be, "Certainly, but not in the manner in which the Spirit of God now resides in the church of Jesus Christ." You read of the prophets and of other gracious men that the Spirit of God came upon them, seized them, moved them, spoke by them, but did not dwell in them. His operations upon men were coming and going. They were carried away by the Spirit of God and came under His power, but the Spirit of God did not rest upon them or abide in them. Occasionally, the sacred endowment of the Spirit of God came upon them, but they knew not "the communion of the Holy Ghost" (2 Cor. 13:14). As a French pastor very sweetly put it:

He [the Holy Spirit] appeared unto men; He did not incarnate Himself in man. His actions were intermittent: He went and came, like the dove which Noah sent forth from the ark and which went to and fro, finding no rest; while in the new dispensation He dwells, He abides in the heart as the dove, His emblem, which John the Baptist saw descending and alighting upon the head of Jesus. Affianced of the soul, the Spirit went off to see His betrothed but was not yet one with her; the marriage was not consummated until the Pentecost after the glorification of Jesus Christ.

You know how our Lord puts it, "He dwelleth with you, and shall be in you" (John 14:17). That indwelling is another thing from being with us. The Holy Spirit was with the apostles in the days when Jesus was with them, but He was not in them in the sense in which He filled them at and after the Day of Pentecost. This shows how intimately the gift of the Holy Spirit is connected with our Lord Jesus Christ, inasmuch as, in the fullest sense of His indwelling, the Holy Spirit would not be with us until Christ had been glorified.

It has been well observed that our Lord sent out seventy evangelists to preach the Gospel (see Luke 10:1), even as He had before that time sent out the twelve. No doubt they preached with great zeal and produced much stir, but the Holy Spirit never took the trouble

to preserve one of their sermons or even the
notes of one. I have not the slightest doubt
that those sermons were very crude and in-
complete, showing more of human zeal than of
divine unction, and hence they are forgotten.
But, no sooner had the Holy Spirit fallen than
Peter's first sermon was recorded, and from
then on we have frequent notes of the utter-
ances of apostles, deacons, and evangelists.
There was an abiding fullness and an overflowing of blessing out of the souls of the saints after the Lord was glorified that was not existing
among men before that time.

Observe, too, that the Holy Spirit was
given after the ascent of our divine Lord into
His glory, partly to make that ascent the more
renowned. "When he ascended up on high, he
led captivity captive, and gave gifts unto men"
(Eph. 4:8). These gifts were men in whom the
Holy Spirit dwelled, who preached the Gospel
to the nations. The shedding of the Holy Spirit
upon the assembled disciples on that memo-
rable day was the glorification of the risen
Christ upon the earth. I know not in what way
the Father could have made the glory of
heaven to flow so effectually from the heights
of the New Jerusalem and to come streaming
down among the sons of men as by giving that
chief of all gifts, the gift of the Holy Spirit,

when the Lord had risen and gone into His glory. With emphasis may I say of the Spirit at Pentecost that He glorified Christ by descending at such a time. What grander celebration could there have been? Heaven rang with hosannas, and earth echoed the joy. The descending Spirit is the noblest testimony among men to the glory of the ascended Redeemer.

Was not the Spirit of God also sent at the time as an evidence of our divine Master's acceptance? Did not the Father thus say to the church, "My Son has finished the work, and has fully entered into his glory; therefore, I give you the Holy Spirit"? If you would know what a harvest is to come of the sowing of the bloody sweat and of the death wounds, see the first fruits. Behold how the Holy Spirit is given: Himself as the first fruits, the earnest of the glory which will yet be revealed in us. I want no better assertion from God of the finished work of Jesus than His blazing, flaming seal of tongues of fire upon the heads of the disciples. He must have done His work, or such a boon as this would not have come from it.

Moreover, if you desire to see how the work of the Spirit comes to us in connection with the work of Christ, recollect that it is the Spirit's work to bear witness of Jesus Christ. He does not take of a thousand different matters and show them to us, but He will "receive of mine," says Christ, "and shall show it unto you" (John 16:14). The Spirit of God is engaged in a service in which the Lord Jesus Christ is the beginning and the end. He comes to men that they may come to Jesus. Hence, He comes to convince us of sin that He may reveal the great sacrifice for sin. He comes to convince us of righteousness, that we may see the righteousness of Christ and of judgment, that we may be prepared to meet Him when He will come "to judge the quick and dead" (1 Pet. 4:5).

It is by the Gospel of Jesus Christ that the Spirit of God works in the hearts of men. "Faith cometh by hearing, and hearing by the word of God" (Rom. 10:17); the Holy Spirit uses the hearing of the Word of God for the conviction, conversion, consolation, and sanctification of men. His usual, ordinary method of operation is to fasten upon the mind the things of God and to put life and force into the consideration of them. He revives in men's memories things that have long been forgotten and frequently makes these the means of affecting the heart and conscience. The men can hardly recollect hearing these truths, but still they heard them at some time or another. Saving truths are such matters as are contained in their substance in the Word of God and lie within the range of the teaching or the person or work or offices of our Lord Jesus Christ. It is the Spirit's one business here below to reveal Christ to us and in us, and to that work He steadily adheres.

Moreover, the Holy Spirit's work is to conform us to the likeness of Jesus Christ. He is not molding us to this or that human ideal, but He is forming us into the likeness of Christ that He may "be the firstborn among many brethren" (Rom. 8:29). Jesus Christ is that standard and model to which the Spirit of God by His sanctifying processes is bringing us, until Christ is formed in us "the hope of glory" (Col. 1:27).

Evermore it is for the glory of Jesus that the Spirit of God works. He works not for the glory of a church or of a community; He works not for the honor of a man or for the distinction of a sect. His one great object is to glorify Christ. "He shall glorify me" (John 16:14) is our Savior's declaration, and when He takes of the things of Christ and shows them to us, we are led more and more to reverence and love and adore our blessed Lord Jesus Christ.

The Operations of the Holy Spirit Are of Incomparable Value

These operations are of such incomparable value that the very best thing we can think of was not thought to be so precious as these are. Our Lord Himself says, "It is expedient for you that I go away: for if I go not away, the Comforter will not come unto you" (John 16:7). Beloved friends, the presence of Jesus Christ was of inestimable value to His disciples, and yet it was not such an advantage to His servants as the indwelling of the Holy Spirit. Is this not a wonderful statement? Well does our Lord preface it by saying, "Nevertheless I tell you the truth" (John 16:7), as if He felt that they would find it a hard saying, for a hard saying it is.

Consider for a moment what Christ was to His disciples while He was here, and then see what must be the value of the Spirit's operations when it was expedient that they should lose all that blessing in order to receive the Spirit of God. Our Lord Jesus Christ was to them their teacher; they had learned everything from His lips. He was their leader; they had never to ask what to do, they had only to follow in His steps. He was their defender; whenever the Pharisees or Sadducees assailed them, He was like a brazen wall to them. He was their comforter; in all times of grief they resorted to Him, and His dear sympathetic heart poured out floods of comfort at once. What if I were to say that the Lord Jesus

Christ was everything to them, their all. What a father is to his children, what a mother is to her suckling, that was Jesus Christ to His disciples; yet the Spirit of God's abiding in the church is better even than all this.

Now consider another thought. What would you think if Jesus Christ were to come among us now as in the days of His flesh—I mean not as He will come but as He appeared at His first advent? What joy it would give you! Oh, the delights, the heavenly joys, to hear that Jesus Christ of Nazareth was on earth again, a man among men! Should we not clap our hands for joy? Our one question would be, "Master, where dwellest thou?" (John 1:38), for we should all long to live just where He lived. We could then sympathize with the former slaves when they flocked into Washington in large numbers to take up their residence there. Why do you think they came to live in that city? Because Abraham Lincoln who had set them free lived there, and they thought it would be glorious to live as near as possible to their great friend.

If Jesus lived anywhere, it would not matter where; if it were in the desert or on the bleakest of mountains, there would be a rush to the place. How the spot would be crowded; what rents they would pay for the worst of tenements if Jesus were but in the neighborhood. But do you not see the difficulty? We could not all get near Him in any literal or bodily fashion. Now that the church is multiplied into millions of believers, some of the Lord's followers would never be able to see Him, and most could only hope to speak with Him now and then. In the days of His flesh, the twelve might see Him every day and so might the little company of disciples, but the case is altered now that multitudes are trusting in His name.

"But," you say, "surely it would thrill the church with enthusiasm." Fancy the Lord Himself standing on your church's platform in the same garb as when He was upon earth. Oh, what rapturous worship! What burning zeal! What enthusiasm! You would go home in such a state of excitement as you never were in before. Yes, it is even so, but then the Lord is not going to carry on His kingdom by the force of mere mental excitement, not even by such enthusiasm as would follow the sight of His person.

The work of the Holy Spirit is a truer work, a deeper work, a surer work, and will more effectually achieve the purposes of God than even would the enthusiasm to which we should be stirred by the bodily presence of our well-beloved Savior. The work is to be spiritual, and therefore the visible presence has departed. It is better that it should be so. We must walk by faith and by faith alone; how could we do this if we could see the Lord with these mortal eyes? This is the dispensation of the unseen Spirit in which we render glory to God by trusting in His Word and relying upon the unseen energy. Now, faith works and faith triumphs though the world sees not the foundation upon which faith is built, for the Spirit who works in us cannot be discerned by carnal minds: "The world...seeth him not, neither knoweth him" (John 14:17).

Thus you see that the operations of the Holy Spirit must be inestimably precious. There is no calculating their value, since it is expedient that we lose the bodily presence of Christ rather than remain without the indwelling of the Spirit of God.

The Operations of the Holy Spirit Are of Marvelous Power

Those operations of the Spirit of God, of which I am afraid some Christians are almost ignorant, are of wondrous power. The text says, "He that believeth on me...out of his belly shall flow rivers of living water" (John

7:38). Fellow believers, do you understand my text? Do rivers of living water flow out of you?

Notice, first, that this is to be an inward work; the rivers of living water are to flow out of the midst of the man. The words are, according to our version, "out of his belly"—that is, from his heart and soul. The rivers do not flow out of his mouth; the promised power is not oratory. We have had plenty of words, floods of words, but this is heart work. The source of the rivers is found in the inner life. It is an inward work at its fountainhead. It is not a work of talent and ability and show and glitter and glare; it is altogether an inward work. The life-flood is to come out of the man's inmost self, out of the bowels and essential being of the man.

Homage is shown too generally to outward form and external observance, though these soon lose their interest and power. But when the Spirit of God rests within a man, it exercises a home rule within him, and he gives great attention to what an old divine was accustomed to call "the home department." Alas, many neglect the realm within which is the chief province under our care. Oh, my friend in Christ, if you would be useful, begin with yourself. It is out of your very soul that a blessing must come. It cannot come out of you if it is not in you, and it cannot be in you unless God the Holy Spirit places it there.

Next, it is life-giving work. Out of the heart of the man, out of the center of his life, are to flow rivers of living water. That is to say, he is instrumentally to communicate to others the divine life. When he speaks, when he prays, when he acts, he will so speak and pray and act that there will be going out of him an emanation which is full of the life of grace and godliness. He will be a light by which others will see. His life will be the means of kindling life in other men's bosoms. "Out of his belly shall flow rivers of living water" (John 7:38).

Note the plenitude of it. The passage would have been a surprising one, if it had said, "Out of him shall flow a river of living water," but it is not so. It says "rivers." Have you ever stood by the side of a very abundant spring? We have some such not far from London. You see the water bubbling up from many little mouths. Observe the sand dancing as the water forces its way from the bottom, and there, just across the road, a mill is turned by the stream which has just been created by the spring. When the waterwheel is turned, you see a veritable river flowing forward to supply Father Thames. Yet this is only one river.

What would you think if you saw a spring yielding such supplies that a river flowed from it to the north, a river to the south, a river to the east, and a river to the west? This is the figure before us: rivers of living water flowing out of the living man in all directions. What a word is this! Rivers of living water! Oh, that all professing Christians were such fountains.

See how spontaneous it is: "Out his belly shall flow." No pumping is required; nothing is said about machinery and hydraulics. The man does not need exciting and stirring up, but, just as he is, influence of the best kind quietly flows out from him. Did you ever hear a great hubbub in the morning, a great outcry, a sounding of trumpets and drums, and did you ever ask, "What is it?" Did a voice reply, "The sun is about to rise, and he is making this noise that all may be aware of it"? No, he shines, but he has nothing to say about it. Likewise, the genuine Christian just goes about flooding the world with blessing; so far from claiming attention for himself, it may be that he himself is unconscious of what he is effecting. God so blesses him that his leaf does not wither, and whatever he does is prospering, for "he shall be like a tree planted by the rivers of water, that bringeth forth his fruit in his season" (Ps. 1:3). His foliage and fruit are the natural outcome of his vigorous life. Oh, the blessed spontaneity of the work of grace when a man gets into the fullness of it, for then he seems to eat and drink and sleep eternal life, and he spreads a savor of salvation all round.

And this is to be perpetual—not like intermittent springs which burst forth and flow in torrents and then cease—but it is to be an everyday outgushing. In summer and winter, by day and by night, wherever the man is, he will be a blessing. As he breathes, he will breathe benedictions; as he thinks, his mind will be devising generous things; and when he acts, his acts will be as though the hand of God were working by the hand of man.

I hope many sighs are rising up from you! I hope friends are saying, "Oh, that I could get to that." I want you to attain the fullness of the favor. I pray that we may all get it. Because Jesus Christ is glorified, therefore the Holy Spirit is given in this fashion, given more largely to those in the kingdom of heaven than to all those holy men before the Lord's ascent to His glory. God gives no stinted blessing to celebrate the triumph of His Son. "God giveth not the Spirit by measure unto him" (John 3:34). On such an occasion, heaven's grandest liberality was displayed. Christ is glorified in heaven above, and God would have Him glorified in the

church below by granting a baptism of the Holy
Spirit to each of us.

These Operations of the Spirit of God Are Easily Obtained by the Lord's Children

Did you say you had not received them?
They are to be had; they are to be had at once.
First, they are to be had by believing in Jesus:
"This spake he of the Spirit, which they that
believe on him should receive" (John 7:39). Do
you not see that it is faith which gives us the
first drink and causes us to live? Do you not
see that this second more abundant blessing of
being ourselves made fountains from which
rivers flow comes in the same way? Believe in
Christ, for the blessing is to be obtained not by
the works of the law, not by so much fasting
and striving and effort, but by belief in the
Lord Jesus for it. With Him is the residue of
the Spirit.

He is prepared to give this to you, yes, to
everyone of you who believe in His name. He
will not, of course, make all of you preachers,
for who then would be hearers? If all were
preachers, the other works of the church
would be neglected. However, He will give
you this favor: out of you there will stream a

divine influence all round you to bless your
children, to bless your servants, to bless the
workmen in the business where you are employed, and to bless the street on which you
live. In proportion as God gives you opportunity, these rivers of living water will flow in
this channel and in that, and they will be
pouring forth from you at all times if you believe in Jesus for the full blessing and can by
faith receive it.

But there is another thing to be done as
well, and that is to pray. Here I want to re-
mind you of those blessed words of the Master:

*Every one that asketh receiveth; and he
that seeketh findeth; and to him that
knocketh it shall be opened. If a son
shall ask bread of any of you that is a father, will he give him a stone? or if he
ask a fish, will he for a fish give him a
serpent? Or if he shall ask an egg, will
he offer him a scorpion? If ye then, being
evil, know how to give good gifts unto
your children: how much more shall
your heavenly Father give the Holy
Spirit to them that ask him?*
(Luke 11:10–13)

You see, there is a distinct promise to the
children of God that their heavenly Father will

give them the Holy Spirit if they ask for His power. That promise is made to be exceedingly strong by the instances joined to it. But He says, "How much more shall your heavenly Father give the Holy Spirit to them that ask him?" He makes it a stronger case than that of an ordinary parent. The Lord must give us the Spirit when we ask Him, for in this He has bound Himself by no ordinary pledge. He has used a metaphor which would bring dishonor on His own name, and that of the very grossest kind, if He did not give the Holy Spirit to them that ask Him.

Oh, then, let us ask Him at once with all our hearts. I pray that some who have never received the Holy Spirit at all may now be led to pray, "Blessed Spirit, visit me; lead me to Jesus." But, especially those of you who are the children of God—to you is this promise especially made. Ask God to make you all that the Spirit of God can make you, not only a satisfied believer who has drunk for himself but a useful believer who overflows the neighborhood with blessing. What a blessing it would be if you went back to your respective churches overflowing, for there are numbers of churches that need flooding. They are dry as a barn floor, and little dew ever falls on them. Oh, that they might be flooded!

What a wonderful thing a flood is! Go down to the river, look over the bridge, and see the barges and other craft lying in the mud. All the king's horses and all the king's men cannot tug them out to sea. There they lie, dead and motionless as the mud itself. What will we do with them? What machinery can move them? Is there a great engineer who will devise a scheme for lifting these vessels and bearing them down to the river's mouth? No, it cannot be done. But, wait until the tide comes in. What a change! Each vessel walks the water like a thing of life. What a difference between the low tide and the high tide. You cannot stir the boats when the water is gone, but when the tide is full, see how readily they move. A little child may push them with his hand.

Oh, for a flood of grace! The Lord send to all our churches a great spring tide! Then the indolent will be active enough, and those who were half dead will be full of energy. I know that in my particular dock are lying several vessels that I should like to float, but I cannot stir them. They neither work for God nor come out to the prayer meetings nor give of their substance to spread the Gospel. If the flood would come, you would see what they are capable of. They would be active, fervent, generous, abounding in every good word and work. So may it be! So may it be!

May springs begin to flow in all our churches, and may all of you get your share of the streams. Oh, that the Lord may now fill you and then send you out, bearing a flood of grace with you. It sounds odd to speak of a man carrying a flood within him. Yet, I hope it will be so, and that out of you will flow "rivers of living water." May God grant it for Jesus' sake. Amen.

Chapter 6

The Abiding of the Spirit

*Yet now be strong, O Zerubbabel, saith the
LORD; and be strong, O Joshua, son of Josedech,
the high priest; and be strong, all ye people of the
land, saith the LORD, and work: for I am with
you, saith the LORD of hosts: According to the
word that I covenanted with you when ye came
out of Egypt, so my spirit remaineth among you:
fear ye not.*
—Haggai 2:4–5

S atan is always doing his utmost to obstruct
the work of God. He hindered these Jews
from building the temple, and today he
endeavors to hinder the people of God from
spreading the Gospel. A spiritual temple is to be
built for the Most High, and if by any means the
evil one can delay its uprising, he will stop at
nothing. If he can take us away from working
with faith and courage for the glory of God, he
will be sure to do it. He is very cunning and
knows how to change his argument and yet
keep to his design. He cares little how he works
so long as he can hurt the cause of God.

In the case of the Jewish people on their return from captivity, he sought to prevent the building of the temple by making them selfish and worldly so that every man was eager to build his own house and cared nothing for the house of the Lord. Each family pleaded its own urgent needs. In returning to a long-deserted and neglected land, much had to be done to make up for lost time; to provide suitably for itself, every family needed all its exertions. They carried this thrift and self-providing to a great extreme and secured for themselves luxuries while the foundations of the temple that had been laid years before remained as they were or became still more thickly covered up with rubbish. The people could not be made to bestir themselves to build a house of God, for they answered to every exhortation, "The time is not come, the time that the LORD'S house should be built" (Hag. 1:2).

A more convenient season was always looming in the future, but it never came. Just now it was too hot; further on it was too cold. At one time, the wet season was just setting in, and it was of no use to begin. Soon after, the fair weather required that they should be in their own fields. Like some in our day, they saw to themselves first, and God's turn was very long in coming. Hence, the prophet cried,

"Is it time for you, O ye, to dwell in your ceiled houses, and this house lie waste?" (Hag. 1:4).

By the mouth of His servant, Haggai, stern rebukes were uttered, and the whole people were aroused. We read,

> *Then Zerubbabel the son of Shealtiel, and Joshua the son of Josedech, the high priest, with all the remnant of the people, obeyed the voice of the LORD their God, and the words of Haggai the prophet, as the LORD their God had sent him, and the people did fear before the LORD.* (Hag. 1:12)

All hands were put to the work, course after course of stone began to rise, and then another stumbling-block was thrown in the way of the workers. The older folks remarked that this was a very small affair compared with the temple of Solomon of which their fathers had told them. In fact, their rising building was nothing at all and not worthy to be called a temple.

The prophet describes the feeling in the verse which precedes our text. "Who is left among you that saw this house in her first glory? and how do ye see it now? is it not in your eyes in comparison of it as nothing?" (Hag. 2:3). Feeling that their work would be very poor and insignificant, the people had little heart to go on. Being discouraged by the humiliating contrast, they began to be slack. As they were quite willing to accept any excuse, and here was an excuse ready-made for them, they would soon have been at a standstill had not the prophet met the wiles of the archenemy with another word from the Lord.

Nothing so confounds the evil one as the voice of the Eternal. Our Lord himself defeated Satan by the Word of the Lord, and the prophet Haggai did the same. Twice the voice was heard: "I am with you, saith the LORD" (Hag. 1:13; 2:4). They were also assured that what they built was accepted and that the Lord meant to fill the new house with glory; yes, He meant to light it up with a glory greater than that which honored the temple of Solomon. They were not spending their strength for naught but were laboring with divine help and favor. Thus, they were encouraged to put their shoulders to the work. The walls rose in due order, and God was glorified in the building up of His Zion.

The present times are, in many respects, similar to those of Haggai. History certainly repeats itself within the church of God as well as outside of it, and therefore the messages of God need to be repeated also. The words of some almost-forgotten prophet may be redelivered by the watchman of the Lord in these present days and be a timely word for the present emergency. We are not free from the worldliness which puts self first and God nowhere, or else our various enterprises would be more abundantly supplied with the silver and the gold that are the Lord's but that even professing Christians reserve for themselves. When this selfish greed is conquered, then comes in a timorous depression. Among those who have escaped from worldliness, there is apt to be too much despondency, and men labor feebly as if working for a cause which is doomed to failure. This last evil must be cured. I pray that our text may flame from the Lord's own mouth with all the fire which once blazed about it. May faint hearts be encouraged and drowsy spirits be aroused as we hear the Lord say, "My spirit remaineth among you: fear ye not" (Hag. 2:5).

I will enter fully upon the subject, by the assistance of the Holy Spirit, by calling your attention to discouragement forbidden. Then I will discuss encouragement imparted. Having done so, I will linger with this blessed text which overflows with comfort and will speak, in the third place, of encouragement further applied. Oh, that our Lord, who knows "how to

speak a word in season to him that is weary"
(Isa. 50:4), may cheer the hearts of seekers by
what will be addressed under this last point of
discourse!

Discouragement Forbidden

Discouragement comes readily enough to
poor mortals like us who are occupied in the
work of God, seeing that it is a work of faith, a
work of difficulty, a work above our capacity,
and a work much opposed. Discouragement is
very natural; it is a native of the soil of man-
hood. To believe is supernatural; faith is the
work of the Spirit of God. To doubt is natural
to fallen men, for we have within us an evil
heart of unbelief. It is abominably wicked, I
grant you, but still it is natural because of the
downward tendency of our depraved hearts.

Discouragement may come and does come
to us, as it did to these people, from a consideration of the great things which God deserves
at our hands and the small things which we
are able to render. When in Haggai's days the
people thought of Jehovah and of a temple for
Him and then looked upon the narrow space
which had been enclosed and the common
stones which had been laid for foundations,
they were ashamed. Where were those hewn

stones and costly stones which, of old, Solomon brought from afar? They said within themselves, "This house is unworthy of Jehovah: what are we doing by laboring thus?" Have you not felt the depressing weight of what is so surely true? Fellow believers, all that we do is little for our God, far too little for Him who loved us and gave Himself for us. For Him that poured out His soul unto death on our behalf, the most splendid service, the most heroic self-denial, are all too little, and we feel it is so. Alabaster boxes of precious ointment are too poor a gift. When we have done our utmost in declaring the glory of Jesus, we have felt that words are too poor and coarse to set before our adorable Lord.

When we have prayed for His kingdom, we have been disgusted with our own prayers, and all the efforts we have put forth in connection with any part of His service have seemed too few, too feeble for us to hope for acceptance. Thus have we been discouraged. The enemy has worked upon us by this means, yet he has made us argue very wrongly. Because we could not do much, we have half resolved to do nothing! Because what we did was so poor, we were inclined to quit the work altogether! This is evidently absurd and wicked. The enemy can use humility for his purpose as well as pride.

Whether he makes us think too much or too little of our work, it is all the same so long as he can get us away from it.

It is significant that the man with one talent went and hid his Lord's money in the earth. He knew that it was but one, and for that reason he was the less afraid to bury it. Perhaps he argued that the interest on one talent could never come to much and would never be noticed side by side with the result of five or ten talents, and he might as well bring nothing at all to his Lord as bring so little. Perhaps he might not have wrapped it up if it had not been so small that a napkin could cover it. The smallness of our gifts may be a temptation to us. We are consciously so weak and so insignificant, compared with the great God and His great cause, that we are discouraged and think it vain to attempt anything.

Moreover, the enemy contrasts our work with that of others and with that of those who have gone before us. We are doing so little as compared to other people; therefore, let us give up. We cannot build like Solomon; therefore, let us not build at all. Yet, fellow believers, there is a falsehood in all this, for, in truth, nothing is worthy of God. The great works of others and even the amazing productions of Solomon all fell short of His glory. What house could man build for God? What are cedar and marble and gold as compared with the glory of the Most High? Though the house was exceedingly magnificent, "of fame and of glory throughout all countries" (1 Chron. 22:5), the Lord God has of old dwelt within curtains, and never was His worship more glorious than within the tent of badgers' skins. Indeed, as soon as the great house was built, true religion declined. What of all human work can be worthy of the Lord? Our little labors do but share the insignificance of greater things, and therefore we ought not to withhold them. Yet, here is the temptation from which we must pray to be delivered.

The tendency to depreciate the present because of the glories of the past is also injurious. The old people looked back to the days of the former temple, even as we are apt to look upon the times of the great preachers of the past. What work was done in those past days! What Sabbaths were enjoyed then! What converts were added to the church! What days of refreshing were then bestowed! Everything has declined, decreased, degenerated!

But, fellow believers, we must not allow this sense of littleness to hamper us, for God can bless our littleness and use it for His glory. I notice that the great men of the past thought of themselves even as we think of ourselves.

Certainly they were not more self-confident than we are. Let us throw our hearts and souls into the work of the Lord and yet do something more nearly in accordance with our highest ideal of what our God deserves of us. Let us excel our ancestors. Let us aspire to be even more godly, more conscientious, and more sound in the faith than they were, for the Spirit of God remains with us.

Wherever discouragement comes in, it is dreadfully weakening. I am sure it is weakening because the prophet was bidden to say three times: "Be strong" (Hag. 2:4), to the governor, high priest, and people. This proves that they had become weak. Being discouraged, their hands hung down, and their knees were feeble. Faith girds us with omnipotence, but unbelief makes everything hang loose and limp about us. Distrust, and you will fail in everything; believe, and "according to your faith be it unto you" (Matt. 9:29). To lend a discouraged people to the Holy War is as difficult as for Xerxes' commanders to conduct the Persian troops to battle against the Greeks. The vassals of the great king were driven to the conflicts by whips and sticks, for they were afraid to fight. Do you wonder that they were defeated? A church that needs constant exhorting and compelling accomplishes nothing. The

Greeks had no need of blows and threats, for each man was a lion and courted the encounter, however great the odds against him. Each Spartan fought *con amore* (with love, devotion); he was never more at home than when contending for the altars and the hearths of his country.

We want Christian men of this same sort, who have faith in their principles, faith in the doctrines of grace, and faith in God the Father, God the Son, and God the Holy Spirit. We want men who therefore contend earnestly for the faith in these days when piety is mocked from the pulpit and the Gospel is sneered at by professional preachers. We need men who love the truth, to whom it is dear as their lives, men into whose hearts the old doctrine is burned by the hand of God's Spirit through a deep experience of its necessity and of its power. We need no more of those who will parrot what they are taught, but we want men who will speak what they know. Oh, for a troop of men like John Knox, heroes of the martyr and covenanter stock! Then would Jehovah of hosts have a people who would "be strong in the Lord, and in the power of His might" (Eph. 6:10) to serve Him.

Discouragement not only weakens men, but it takes them away from the service of

God. It is significant that the prophet said to them, "Be strong, all ye people of the land, saith the LORD, and work" (Hag. 2:4). They had ceased to build; they had begun to talk and argue, but they had laid down the trowel. They were extremely wise in their observations and criticisms and prophecies, but the walls did not rise. It is always so when we are discouraged; we cease from the work of the Lord and waste time in talk and nonsensical refinements. May the Lord take away discouragement from any of you who now suffer from it. I suppose some of you feel it, for at times it creeps over my heart and makes me go with heaviness to my work.

I believe that God's truth will come to the front yet, but it has many adversaries today. All sorts of unbeliefs are being hatched out from under the wings of "modern thought." The Gospel seems to be regarded as a nose of wax, to be altered and shaped by every man who wishes to show his superior skill. Nor is it in doctrine alone, but in practice also, that the times are out of joint. Separateness from the world and holy living have given way to gaiety and theatergoing. To follow Christ fully has gone out of fashion with many of those from whom we once hoped better things. Yet are there some who waver not, some who are willing to be in the right with two or three. Blessed is the man who will be able to stand fast by his God in these evil days. Let us not in any way be discouraged. "Be strong...be strong ...be strong" (Hag. 2:4) sounds as a threefold voice from the triune God. "Fear ye not" (Hag. 2:5) comes as a sweet cordial to the faint; therefore, let no man's heart fail him.

The Encouragement Imparted

"According to the word that I covenanted with you when ye came out of Egypt, so my spirit remaineth among you: fear ye not" (Hag. 2:5). God remembers His covenant and stands on His ancient promises. When the people came out of Egypt, the Lord was with them by His Spirit; hence, He spoke to them by Moses, and through Moses, He guided and judged and taught them. He was with them also by His Spirit in inspiring Bezaleel and Aholiab as to the works of art which adorned the tabernacle. God always finds workmen for His work and by His Spirit fits them for it. The Spirit of God rested upon the elders who were ordained to relieve Moses of his great burden.

The Lord was also with His people in the fiery cloudy pillar which was conspicuous in the midst of the camp. His presence was their glory and their defense. This is a type of the presence of the Spirit with the church. At the present time, if we hold to the truth of God, if we live in obedience to His holy commands, if we are spiritually minded, if we cry unto God in believing prayer, and if we have faith in His covenant and in His Son, the Holy Spirit abides among us. The Holy Spirit descended upon the church at Pentecost, and He has never gone back again. There is no record of the Spirit's return to heaven. He will abide with the true church evermore. This is our hope for the present struggle. The Spirit of God remains with us.

To what end, my brothers and sisters, is this Spirit with us? Let us think of this, that we may be encouraged at this time. The Spirit of God remains among you to aid and assist the ministry which He has already given. Oh, that the prayers of God's people would always go up for God's ministers, that they may speak with a divine power and influence which none will be able to contradict! We look too much for clever men; we seek out fluent and flowery speakers; we sigh for men cultured and trained in all the knowledge of the heathen. However, if we sought more for unction, for divine authority, and for that power which does hedge about the man of God, how much wiser should we be! Oh, that all of us who profess to preach the Gospel would learn to speak in entire dependence upon the direction of the Holy Spirit, not daring to utter our own words but even trembling lest we should do so. Oh, that we would commit ourselves to that secret influence without which nothing will be powerful upon the conscience or converting to the heart.

Do you not know the difference between the power that comes from human oratory and that which comes by the divine energy which speaks so to the heart that men cannot resist it? We have forgotten this too much. It is better to speak six words in the power of the Holy Spirit than to preach seventy years of sermons without the Spirit. He who rested on those who have gone to their reward in heaven can rest this day upon our ministers and bless our evangelists if we will but seek it of Him. Let us cease to grieve the Spirit of God and look to Him for help for the faithful ministers who are yet spared to us.

This same Spirit who of old gave to His church eminent teachers can raise up other and more useful men. The other day, a brother from Wales told me of the great men he remembered. He said that he had never heard such a one as Christmas Evans who surpassed all men when he was in the *hwyl*. I asked him if he knew another Welsh minister who preached like Christmas Evans. "No," he said, "we have no such man in Wales in our days." So also in England, we have neither Wesley nor Whitefield nor any of their order, yet as God is the residue of the Spirit, He can fetch out from some chimney-corner another Christmas Evans or find in our Sunday school another George Whitefield who will declare the Gospel with the Holy Spirit sent down from heaven.

Let us never fear for the future or despair for the present since the Spirit of God remains with us. What if the growing error of the age should have silenced the last tongue that speaks out the old Gospel? Let not faith be weakened. I hear the tramp of legions of soldiers of the Cross. I hear the clarion voices of hosts of preachers. "The Lord gave the word: great was the company of those that published it" (Ps. 68:11). Have faith in God through our Lord Jesus Christ! When He ascended on high, "He led captivity captive, and gave gifts unto men" (Eph. 4:8). He then "gave some, apostles; and some, prophets; and some, evangelists; and some, pastors and teachers" (Eph. 4:11), and He can do the like again. Let us fall back upon the eternal God and never be discouraged for an instant.

Nor is this all. The Holy Spirit being with us, He can move the whole church to exercise its varied ministries. This is one of the things we want very much, that every member of the church should recognize that he is ordained to service. Everyone in Christ, man or woman, has some testimony to bear, some warning to give, some deed to do, in the name of the holy child Jesus; and if the Spirit of God is poured out upon our young men and women, each one will be aroused to energetic service. Both small and great will be in earnest, and the result upon the slumbering masses of our population will surprise us all.

Sometimes we lament that the churches are so dull. There is an old proverb which says of So-and-so that he was "as sound asleep as a church." I suppose there is nothing that can sleep so soundly as a church. Yet, the Spirit of God still remains, and therefore churches can be awakened. I mean that not only in part but as a whole a church may be quickened. The dullest professor, the most slovenly believer, or the most critical and useless member of a church may yet be turned to good account. I see them like a bundle of sticks, piled up, dead, and dry. Oh, for the fire! We will have a blaze out of them yet.

Come, Holy Spirit, heavenly Dove, brood over the dark, disordered church as once You did over chaos; order will come out of confusion, and the darkness will fly before the light.

Only let the Spirit be with us, and we have all that is wanted for victory. Give us His presence, and everything else will come in its due season for the profitable service of the entire church.

If the Spirit is with us, there will come abundant conversions. We cannot get at "the lapsed masses," as they are pedantically called. We cannot stir the crass infidelity of the present age. No, we cannot, but He can. "With God all things are possible" (Matt. 19:26). If you walk down to our bridges at a certain hour of the day, you will see barges and vessels lying in the mud, and nothing can stir them. Wait until the tide comes in, and they will walk the water like things of life. The living flood accomplishes at once what no mortals can do.

And so today our churches cannot stir. What will we do? Oh, that the Holy Spirit would come with a flood tide of His benign influence, as He will if we will but believe in Him, as He must if we will but cry unto Him, and as He will if we will cease to grieve Him. Everything will be even as the saints desire when the Lord of Saints is with us. The hope of the continuance and increase of the church lies in the Spirit remaining with us. The hope of the salvation of London or any other city lies in the wonder-working Spirit. Let us bow our heads and worship the omnipotent Spirit who deigns to work in us, by us, and with us.

Then, fellow believers, if this should happen—and I do not see why it should not—then we may expect to see the church put on her beautiful garments. Then will she begin to clear herself of the errors which now defile her; then will she press to her bosom the truths which she now begins to forget; then will she go back to the pure fount of inspiration and drink from the Scriptures of truth; and then out of the midst of her will flow no turbid streams but "rivers of living water" (John 7:38). If the Holy Spirit will work among us, we will rejoice in the Lord and glory in the name of our God.

When once the Spirit of God puts forth His might, all things else will be in accord with Him. Notice that in the rest of the chapter— not relating to that temple at all but to the church of God—there is great comfort given to us. If the Holy Spirit is given once, then we may expect Providence to cooperate with the church of God. "Yet once, it is a little while, and I will shake the heavens, and the earth, and the sea, and the dry land; And I will shake all nations" (Hag. 2:6–7). Great commotions will cooperate with the Holy Spirit. We may expect that God will work for His people in an extraordinary fashion if they will but be faithful to Him. Empires will collapse and times will change for the truth's sake. Expect the unexpected; reckon upon that which is unlikely, if it is necessary for the growth of the kingdom. Of old the earth helped the woman when the dragon opened his mouth to drown her with the floods that he cast forth (see Revelation 12:16); unexpected help will come to us when affairs are at their worst.

And next, the Lord in this chapter promises His people that they will have all the supplies they need for His work. They feared that they could not build His house because of their poverty, but, says the Lord of Hosts, "The silver is mine, and the gold is mine" (Hag. 2:8). When the church of God believes in God and goes forward bravely, she need not trouble as to supplies. Her God will provide for her. He that gives the Holy Spirit will give gold and silver accordingly as they are needed; therefore, let us be of good courage. If God is with us, why need we fear?

One of our English kings once threatened the great city of London that if its councilors talked so independently, he would—yes, he would, indeed he would—take his court away from the city. The Lord Mayor on that occasion replied that if His Majesty would graciously leave the river Thames behind him, the citizens would try to get on without his court. If any say, "If you hold to these old-fashioned doctrines, you will lose the educated, the wealthy, the influential," we will answer, "But if we do not lose the godly and the presence of the Holy Spirit, we are not in the least alarmed." If the Holy Spirit remains with us, "there is a river, the streams whereof shall make glad the city of God" (Ps. 46:4). Fellow believers, my heart leaps within me as I cry, "The LORD of hosts is with us; the God of Jacob is our refuge" (Ps. 46:7, 11). "Therefore will not we fear, though the earth be removed, and though the mountains be carried into the midst of the sea" (Ps. 46:2).

The best comfort of all remained: "The desire of all nations shall come" (Hag. 2:7). This was in a measure fulfilled when Jesus came into that latter house and caused all holy hearts to sing for gladness, but it was not wholly fulfilled in that way, for if you notice in Haggai 2:9 it is written, "The glory of this latter house shall be greater than of the former...and in this place will I give peace," which the Lord did not fully do to the second temple since that was destroyed by the Romans.

However, there is another advent, when "the desire of all nations shall come" (Hag. 2:7) in power and glory, and this is our highest hope. Though truth may be driven back and error may prevail, Jesus comes, and He is the great Lord and Patron of Truth. "With righteousness shall he judge the world, and the people with equity" (Ps. 98:9). Here is our last resource; here are God's reserves. He whom we serve lives and reigns forever and ever, and He says, "Behold, I come quickly; and my reward is with me, to give every man according as his work shall be" (Rev. 22:12). "Therefore, my beloved brethren, be ye steadfast, unmoveable, always abounding in the work of the Lord, forasmuch as ye know that your labour is not in vain in the Lord" (1 Cor. 15:58).

Encouragement Further Applied

I would be done if it had not been that this text seemed to me to overflow so much that it might not only refresh God's people but give drink to thirsty sinners who are seeking the Lord. It is at the beginning of every gracious purpose that men have most fear, even as these people had who had newly begun to build. When first the Holy Spirit begins to strive with a man and to lead him to Jesus, he is apt to say, "I cannot; I dare not; it is impossible. How can I believe and live?" Now I want to speak to some of you who are willing to find Christ and to encourage you by the truth that the Spirit lives to help you. I would even like to speak to those who are not anxious to be saved.

I remember that Dr. Payson, an exceedingly earnest and useful man of God, once did a singular thing. He had been holding inquiry meetings with all sorts of people, and great numbers had been saved. At last, one Sunday, he publicized that he should have a meeting on Monday night for those people who did not desire to be saved. Strange to say, some twenty people came who did not wish to repent or believe. He spoke to them and said, "I am sure that if a little film, thin as the web of the gossamer, were let down by God from heaven to each one of you, you would not push it away from you. Although it were almost invisible, you would value even the slightest connection between you and heaven. Now, your coming to meet me tonight is a little link with God. I want it to increase in strength until you are joined to the Lord forever." He spoke to them most tenderly, and God blessed those people

who did not desire to be saved so that, before
the meeting was over, they were of another
mind. The film had become a thicker thread,
and it grew and grew until the Lord Christ
held them by it forever.

Dear friends, the fact of your reading this
discussion is like that filmy thread; do not put
it away. Here is your comfort: the Holy Spirit
still works with the preaching of the Word. Do
I hear you say, "I cannot feel my need of Christ
as I want to feel it?" The Spirit remains among
us. He can make you feel more deeply the guilt
of sin and your need of pardon. "But I have
heard so much about conviction and repentance; I do not seem to have either of them."
Yet the Spirit remains with us, and that Spirit
is able to work in you the deepest conviction
and the truest repentance. "Oh, sir, I do not
feel as if I could do anything." But, the Spirit
remains with us, and all things that are needed
for godliness He can give. He can work "in you
both to will and to do of his good pleasure"
(Phil. 2:13). "But I want to believe in the Lord
Jesus Christ unto eternal life." Who made you
want to do that? Who but the Holy Spirit?
Therefore, He is still at work with you, and
though as yet you do not understand what believing is—or else I am persuaded you would
believe at once—the Spirit of God can instruct

you in it. You are blind, but He can give you sight. You are paralyzed, but He can give you strength. The Spirit of God remains.

"Oh, but that doctrine of regeneration staggers me; you know, we must be born again." Yes, we are born again of the Spirit, and the Spirit remains still with us. He is still mighty to work that wondrous change and to bring you out of the kingdom of Satan into the kingdom of God's dear Son. The Spirit remains with us, blessed be His name! "Ah, dear sir," says one, "I want to conquer sin!" Who made you desire to conquer sin? Who, but the Spirit that remains with us? He will give you the sword of the Spirit and teach you how to use it, and He will give you both the will and the power to use it successfully. Through the Spirit's might you can overcome every sin, even that which has dragged you down and disgraced you. The Spirit of God is still waiting to help you.

When I think of the power of the Spirit of God, I look hopefully upon every sinner I see. I bless His name that He can work in you all that is pleasing in His sight. Some of you may be very careless, but He can make you thoughtful. I hope you may yourselves become an exhibition of divine grace. You think not about things, but He can make you feel at this moment a sweet softness stealing over you until you long to be alone and to get in the old armchair and there seek the Lord. You can thus be led to salvation.

Wherever you come from, I want you now to seek the Lord. He has brought you to this point, and He means to bless you. Yield yourselves to Him while His sweet Spirit pleads with you. While the heavenly wind softly blows upon you, open wide every window. You have not felt that you wanted it, but that is the sure proof that you need it, for he that does not know his need of Christ is most in need. Open wide your heart that the Spirit may teach you your need. Above all, breathe the prayer that He would help you right now to look to the Lord Jesus Christ, for there is life in a look at the Crucified One; there is life at this moment for you.

"Oh," you say, "if I were to begin, I should not keep on." No, if you began, perhaps you would not, but if *He* begins with *you*, He will keep on. The final perseverance of saints is the result of the final perseverance of the Holy Spirit. He perseveres to bless, and we persevere in receiving the blessing. If He begins, you have begun with a divine power that "fainteth not, neither is weary" (Isa. 40:28). I wish it might so happen that not the prophet Haggai but I, God's servant, may have written to you such a word as you will never forget. And, may the Lord add to the word by the witness of the Holy Spirit, "From this day will I bless you" (Hag. 2:19). Go with that promise resting upon you.

I would like to give a shake of the hand to every stranger reading this and say, "Brother, in the name of the Lord, I wish you from this day a blessing." Amen and amen.